FLASHBACKS NO. 15

The Flashback series is sponsored by the
European Ethnological Research Centre,
c/o the Royal Museums of Scotland,
Chambers Street, Edinburgh EH1 1JF.

General Editor: Alexander Fenton

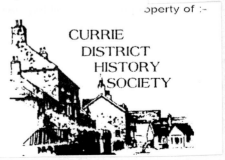

Other titles in the Flashback series include:

ONION JOHNNIES

Personal recollections by nine
French Onion Johnnies of their
working lives in Scotland

Ian MacDougall

TUCKWELL PRESS
in association with
The Scottish Working People's History Trust
and
The European Ethnological Research Centre

First published in Great Britain in 2002 by
Tuckwell Press
The Mill House
Phantassie
East Linton
East Lothian EH40 3DG
Scotland

ISBN 1 86232 220 1

British Library Cataloguing in Publication Data
A catalogue record for this book is available
on request from the British Library

Typeset by Hewer Text Ltd, Edinburgh
Printed and bound by
Bell and Bain Ltd, Glasgow

CONTENTS

ILLUSTRATIONS

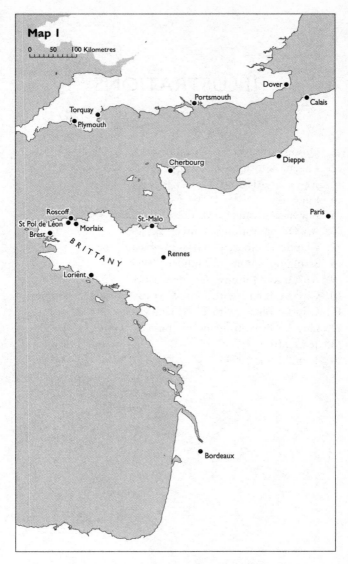

France and the English Channel

Scotland

INTRODUCTION

For almost 150 years until the late twentieth century French Onion Johnnies – or Ingan Johnnies, as they were usually known north of the Border – were a familiar group of seasonal immigrant workers in cities and towns throughout Scotland and indeed Britain. At the beginning of the twenty-first century only one, so far as is known, is still at work in Scotland. He is Yves Rolland, based in Leith, and he and the only other eight known surviving Johnnies (or seven Johnnies and one Onion 'Jenny', Madame Anna Gourlet) who worked in Scotland at one time or another between the 1920s and the 1970s present in the pages below their spoken recollections of their working lives.

Their recollections were recorded in interviews in Leith and in Brittany in 1999 by the Scottish Working People's History Trust. The project was part of the Trust's commitment to gathering the oral recollections of working men and women about their working lives in Scotland, and also about their educational, housing, recreational, and other experiences, and to publishing them in edited form. Three volumes of such recollections – by Roslin, Midlothian, gunpowder mill and bomb factory workers, by bondagers (south-east of Scotland women farm workers), and by Leith dockers – have already been published by the Trust. Many other volumes are in various stages of preparation. They include recollections by miners, journalists, railway workers, Penicuik paper mill workers, Hebridean and north-west Highland crofters, fishermen and others, Borders men farm workers, Leith seamen, public librarians, Co-operative society workers, Peeblesshire textile mill workers, Sutherland and Caithness farmers and fishermen, and building trade workers. To gather and publish in edited form such oral recollections by working men and women is, the Trust believes, a task both important and urgent if hitherto often unexplored aspects of the history of Scotland within living memory and of its working men and women and their organisations are to become generally available and accessible.

About the Onion Johnnies, scores of whom formerly came every year as seasonal workers to sell their onions in Scotland, relatively little has ever been published, except for occasional paragraphs or photographs in newspapers. What distinguishes the nine accounts in the pages below is that they are the Johnnies' own spoken recollections of their years of working in Scotland.

Five of the nine began working as Onion Johnnies between the First and Second World Wars (even if, in the case of François Perron, only for the month before the the outbreak of the Second War in September 1939); the other four began as Johnnies only in the 1950s (or in Claude Quimerch's case, in 1949–50).

Several of these nine Johnnies (or eight Johnnies and one 'Jenny') began selling onions in Scotland as mere children. Thus Jean Saout, the oldest of the nine and now nearing the age of 90, first came with his father to sell onions in Glasgow in 1921 at the age of eight. Jean Milin first arrived as an onion-seller in Leith as a twelve-year-old boy during his school holidays in 1929. That was the age also at which Eugène Guyader, having newly left school, first crossed the English Channel from his home in Brittany to become an Onion Johnny. Anna Gourlet appears to have been slightly younger even than either Eugène Guyader or Jean Milin when, as she recalls, at the age of 11½ or so she accompanied her mother in 1930 or 1931 on the long journey by Channel ferry and train to Leith to become a working member of her father's onion business there.

The others of the nine were older when they became Onion Johnnies. Anna Gourlet's brother François Perron, who was six years younger than she and who had begun school in Leith at the age of seven in 1932, did not, as has been mentioned, become an Onion Johnny there until he was fourteen – and then only for a month or so because of the outbreak of the Second World War and the return then or within a few weeks of all the Johnnies to France. Monsieur Perron returned, however, to Leith as a Johnny after the War in 1949, when he was 23. Yves Rolland, the youngest of these nine Johnnies, began work in Leith in 1959 at the age of 14½. The school-leaving age in Scotland then being 15, it was hardly surprising that his boss or *patron* warned him: 'If you ever get stopped by the police, if they ask what age you are you say 15.' None of the other two or three, however, of these Johnnies who between the Wars began selling onions at even more tender years appears to have recollections of such warnings or of encounters with the police or other authorities on the matter of their age. Jean-Marie Tanguy, whose father's onion-selling business was based in Dundee, recalls attending school there at the age of six or seven in 1935–6, although also because of the disruption caused by the Second World War he did not himself become an Onion Johnny in that city until he was 21 in 1951. Claude Quimerch and Guy Le Bihan, like Jean-Marie Tanguy, were also in their twenties when they became Onion Johnnies at respectively Glasgow in 1949–50 and Ayr in 1957.

For several of the nine the occupation of Onion Johnny was virtually an hereditary one. 'There were,' says Jean-Marie Tanguy, 'four generations of us Onion Johnnies in my family.' From around the middle of the nineteenth century his great-grandfather had been an Onion Johnny at Dundee, his grandfather sold onions there from about 1880, and his father likewise from an early age before the 1914–18 War. Eugène

Guyader was at least a third-generation Johnny, and three of his uncles, as well as the wife of one of them and his own brother, were similarly employed. Second-generation Johnnies at least were Jean Saout, whose father had first gone to sell onions in Britain at the age of 10 or 11 in the 1880s, and also Anna Gourlet and her brother François Perron, as well as Claude Quimerch. On the other hand, of the nine below the remaining three – Jean Milin, Guy Le Bihan, and Yves Rolland – were evidently first-generation Johnnies, although Guy Le Bihan's father-in-law was one and it was he who persuaded Monsieur Le Bihan to join him at Ayr in 1957.

Those three (Jean Milin, Guy Le Bihan, and Yves Rolland) of the nine whose fathers were never themselves Onion Johnnies recall that they nonetheless worked on the land either as small farmers (in the case of both Milin and Le Bihan *père* or senior – and also as a fisherman, in the case of Jean Milin's father) or, in the case of Yves Rolland's father, as a farm worker. The only one among the fathers or grandfathers of the families of the nine Johnnies who is recalled as having been a craftsman is Yves Rolland's paternal grandfather, who was a clog maker.

Only two or perhaps three (Jean Milin, Claude Quimerch, and possibly Yves Rolland) of the nine Johnnies appear when young to have had an ambition to work other than as Onion Johnnies or on the land as a means of helping their parents. Jean Milin wanted to become a merchant seaman, Claude Quimerch a naval officer. The former succeeded in becoming a seaman – but, because of the coming of the Second World War, not in the merchant navy but as a regular in the French navy. Claude Quimerch, as the oldest in a family of six children, had at the age of sixteen to abandon his studies at college (where among other subjects he was learning English, Latin, Greek, German and Spanish) and become the breadwinner as a lorry driver when his father became ill and soon afterwards died. The ambition of Yves Rolland as a boy, influenced, it appears, by his reading of comics, was to come to Scotland. It was as an Onion Johnny that he came aged 14½ – and more than 40 years later he is the only one of the nine Johnnies below who continues to sell onions and other vegetables in Scotland.

Of the occupations before marriage of the mothers of these nine Johnnies, most are recalled. Five of them (the mothers of Jean Milin, Anna Gourlet and her brother François Perron, as well as of Eugène Guyader, Jean-Marie Tanguy and Guy Le Bihan) appear as daughters of small farmers to have worked in their fathers' fields. Yves Rolland's mother was employed as a baker's roundswoman. After marriage the mothers of Anna Gourlet and François Perron and of Jean-Marie Tanguy worked with their husbands in their onion-selling businesses at respectively Leith and Dundee. The mothers of Jean Saout and Claude Quimerch died when both were infants.

Premature death indeed stalks several of the recollections below. Eugène Guyader's father lost his first wife while he was away fighting in the 1914–18 War, which claimed the lives also of two of his five brothers. The death of Monsieur Guyader's own young son in 1957 was a factor that resulted in his transferring his work as an Onion Johnny from the south of England to Glasgow. Guy Le Bihan's grandfather and one of Claude Quimerch's uncles were killed in the 1914–18 War.

As the only seasonal immigrant onion sellers in Britain, Onion Johnnies all came from a relatively small area of Brittany. As Yves Rolland puts it: 'There weren't onion sellers like us Johnnies who came from Spain or Poland to sell their onions. The only Onion Johnnies were from Brittany.' It was from the English Channel port of Roscoff and its small neighbouring towns or villages such as St Pol de Léon, Plouescat and Santec and their surrounding farms that the Johnnies and their onions came. Of the nine veteran Johnnies who present their recollections in the pages below, four (Anna Gourlet and her brother François Perron, Eugène Guyader and Jean-Marie Tanguy) belong to Roscoff, two (Jean Saout and Yves Rolland) to St Pol de Léon, two others (Guy Le Bihan and apparently Claude Quimerch) to Santec, and Jean Milin to Plouescat.

The recollections by these nine veterans make no claim, of course, to constitute an objective, systematic or comprehensive history of Onion Johnnies in Scotland. They are their personal recollections of their work and other experiences in the various towns and areas of Scotland where they were based and where they sold their onions. While a scholarly history of the Onion Johnnies in Scotland has yet to be written, it appears that the origins of the yearly journeys to there and elsewhere in Britain by the Johnnies and their cargoes of *oignons rosés* or pink onions have to be sought in the decade or more after the Napoleonic Wars had ended in 1815 at Waterloo. Eugène Guyader refers to the first Johnnies setting out from Santec in 1828 to cross the Channel to sell onions in Britain, while Yves Rolland recalls his *patron* or boss at Leith telling him the traffic arose out of the rescue from drowning at Roscoff of British royal personages and the consequent grant of permission to local people to sell their onions on the other side of the Channel. Whatever the origins, Monsieur Rolland says: 'We didn't need to apply for a licence to sell onions. We have an Association in Brittany and it gives you freedom to come and trade in this country with onions, garlic and shallots. So we didn't have to apply to Edinburgh Town Council for a licence. We never had any kind of licence.' François Perron, in expressing a similar view, adds: 'I think it was the parliament in London which gave the Onion Johnnies the licence to sell their onions in Britain. The Johnnies' job was special. It was authorised in that way.'

Whatever and whenever the origins of the Johnnies' annual

migration across the Channel to England, Wales and Scotland,[1] it took place regularly toward the end of July and in early August. 'In those days,' recalls Jean Saout of his first journey with his father in 1921 at the age of eight to sell onions in Glasgow, 'the onions were ready sooner than they are nowadays . . . So normally when I was young the Onion Johnnies went to Britain in the month of July to begin the season of selling the onions. The Pardon – a Breton religious festival – took place on the 15th or 16th of July. So the Johnnies set off from home about ten days later.' François Perron, a younger and later Johnny, recalls that '. . . from 1949 onwards we went to Leith every August for the onion-selling season.'

Most of the Johnnies, at least in the twentieth century, appear to have travelled to Scotland from Brittany by Channel ferry and train. When, aged 11½, Anna Gourlet first went in 1930 or 1931 with her mother to Leith to work in her father's onion-selling business there, they went by train while her father sailed from Roscoff to Leith with the cargo of onions. 'I was very excited,' Madame Gourlet recalls. 'We went from Roscoff to Paris on the train, then from Paris to Dieppe. We took the ferry across the Channel from Dieppe to Newhaven. That took about four hours, I think. And then the train again from Newhaven to London, and from London to Edinburgh. Oh, it was a long journey, but I wasn't tired out! . . . And I wasn't seasick at all. The sea was quite calm.' Several others among these nine Johnnies recall similar annual journeys to Scotland, sometimes by varying routes. The two days and a night spent in travelling from Roscoff to Leith recalled by Yves Rolland on his first journey in 1959 at the age of 14½ were enlivened by the determination of some of the older Johnnies to pay frequent tribute en route to Bacchus. Jean Milin, on the other hand, was, like Anna Gourlet's father, a Johnny who sailed with the onions from Roscoff to Scotland. 'It was a small boat,' he recalls of his first such voyage in 1929 when he was 12 years old, 'a sailing boat with no motors and no nothing at all! It took us fifteen days to sail from Roscoff to Leith because the weather was bad. The sails of the boat were torn twice by the winds. But a small British boat came and took us into the port of Leith . . . But I wasn't seasick on that voyage. I was already accustomed to sailing . . . It was always my wish to sail. Every year after that I went with the boat with the onions from Roscoff to Leith, because I liked the sea, I liked it so much.' 'The first time I went, in 1934,' recalls Eugène Guyader, 'we were all nine or ten of us in the boat that took the onions from Roscoff to Torquay. It was small, 20 or 25 tons, like a fishing boat . . . Oh, there were so many boats that were going to England, and we all left about the same time – in the middle of July.'

Once arrived in Scotland, the Onion Johnnies generally worked in the first half of the twentieth century either in companies varying in numbers from half a dozen to almost a score of men, youths and even mere boys, or in some cases in smaller family groups, as Anna Gourlet, her parents and her brother François Perron did. They lived at and worked from fixed bases in Glasgow, Leith, Dundee, Aberdeen, Ayr, and several other towns that are mentioned in these recollections. None of the nine Johnnies in the pages below worked in Scotland before the 1914–18 War but several of them did so between the two World Wars. Their testimonies make it clear that living and working conditions in their bases in those years were usually distinctly Spartan. The bases were generally, in the 1920s and '30s, old shops. 'At Leith,' Anna Gourlet recalls of the years she worked there in the 1930s, 'my mother and father had a shop which was also our home in Quality Street. Later on we were at No. 8 Bernard Street. But at Quality Street it was a very simple place. There was really nothing there to begin with. But we managed to store the onions there and to sleep there, too. There weren't any separate rooms in the place in Quality Street: it was a shop, a store place. You made rooms by building up the sacks of onions as walls . . . There was no toilet, nothing, in the shop in Quality Street. The 'toilet' was in the 'room' made with the sacks of onions. I don't remember clearly what water supply there was but there must have been a tap. We slept on the floor to begin with and then later on there were iron bedsteads.' A decade earlier, when Jean Saout, aged 8, first arrived in Glasgow to work with the onions, he recalls that '. . . we lived in a shop in Kingston Street, near the Central Station and near the River Clyde. You used to hear all day, oh, all day, bbbbbrrrrrhhhhh, bbbbbrrrrrhhhhh – hammering and banging of metal as ships were being built on the river. It was a big shop. You slept there, too. My father and I and all the Onion Johnnies slept there. There were perhaps eight or nine Johnnies and perhaps about six bosses, too – *patrons* . . . We had trunks to keep our clothes and things in. But there weren't any beds. We slept on straw and we had blankets to cover ourselves with. It was only on Sundays we shook up the straw with a pitch fork. And then we carried on sleeping on it. You had pillows, too. They were filled with hay. Sometimes you had bits of straw that marked your face when you slept. But you slept well, you slept well.' At Leith, where at the age of 13 in 1930 he began working full-time as an Onion Johnny, Jean Milin found himself a member of a company of nine or ten Johnnies whose base was a shop on three floors at No. 18 Quality Street. 'There were no beds – only straw,' he recalls. 'We all slept together in a row on the straw, like herrings or sardines! I was the youngest and I was in the middle of the row. You had covers, blankets. But we also had a sack or bag to sleep in – a sleeping bag. Oh, it was very comfortable. We were there all together, quite warm in the straw, so we didn't feel cold . . . Then you had a little table to eat on. The kitchen was quite small. There was a tap with running water, and there was a wc downstairs – a flush toilet.' Living and working conditions in such bases appear to have improved in the course of the 1930s and particularly after the 1939–45 War, when the Johnnies returned to work in Scotland and elsewhere in Britain. Jean Saout, for example, still based with the other Johnnies in his company in Kingston Street, Glasgow, recounts how after the war beds or bunks in tiers had replaced the earlier straw for sleeping on, the onions were stored in a room separate from where the Johnnies slept, and there was a small cooking place or kitchen, as well as a wc and sink. Nonetheless conditions for many or most Johnnies seem to have remained rather basic. Yves Rolland recalls how the base in Maritime Street, Leith, of the company of Johnnies where he was employed as a teenager in the early 1960s, was 'a sort of front shop . . . maybe 15 or 16 feet long. And behind it we used to have a wee kitchen, where we used to do our cooking or washing and everything. The shop was full of onions. So at that time we slept in very cramped conditions. Have you ever had rats running on top of you? Well, that's what we had in that shop in Maritime Street. . . I remember there was an old Ingan Johnny . . . [who] . . . used to snore in his bed. This night he was snoring – and this rat was in the bed beside him! You could see everything . . . But at Maritime Street we slept among the onions.'

The companies, particularly in the first half of the twentieth century, were composed generally of a majority of ordinary rank-and-file Johnnies or *ouvriers*, but also of one or two, and in the larger companies up to perhaps half a dozen, bosses or *patrons*. Some of the rank-and-file Johnnies were sons, nephews, or brothers of one or other of the bosses. Thus Jean Saout when he began work as a rank-and-file Onion Johnny in Glasgow in the 1920s was the son of one of about six bosses in charge of the company which employed him. Jean Saout himself became a boss of a company in Glasgow after the 1939–45 War. Jean Milin, on the other hand, for the six or seven years he worked as an Onion Johnny at Leith in the 1930s remained always an *ouvrier*. An *ouvrier* who worked for some years as a rank-and-file John-ny, who could somehow manage to save enough from his wages, who might additionally be fortunate enough to rent or own a small farm in Brittany where he could grow his own onions for sale in Scotland, and who might have the further good fortune to have a father or uncle who was an onion company boss, might himself eventually become a boss or *patron*. It seems likely, however, that at least in the first half of the twentieth century, when there were more Johnnies at work in Scotland and more competition among them than became the case from about the 1960s, most Johnnies re-mained *ouvriers* during their working lives. In the small family companies, such as that headed by the father of Anna Gourlet and François Perron, it was no doubt far more likely that the son would in due course succeed his father as head or *patron*. For any Johnny who, like one nicknamed Pencolo or *Tête de Paille* (Strawhead) based in Glasgow and mentioned below by Guy Le Bihan, branched out on his own it was not easy to make a living. As Monsieur Le Bihan emphasises: 'It wasn't common for Onion Johnnies to work on their own. It wasn't easy to make a living out of selling the onions if you were on your own. Once you finished work selling them you had to come home and make the strings yourself. You didn't have a division of labour, where one Johnny or more sold the onions, and another or others were stringing them in the shop. You really had to have a worker, *un ouvrier*, who strung the onions all day long, preparing them for the sellers to go out the next day and sell them.'

There are frequent references in these nine testimonies to the stringing of the onions, and the important task (carried out usually, it seems, on Sundays) of gathering rushes, straw or hay from nearby fields to form the strings. The numbers and weight of onions in a string (*ficelle*) or bunch (*botte*) are also discussed, as is the skilful way the bunches were formed. 'When you made a bunch of onions you started it with the big onions and after that the small onions, then big ones again. That made the bunch prettier, more attractive for commercial reasons,' recalls Jean Saout. It was such strings and bunches festooned over the handlebars and rear wheels of their bicycles that made the Onion Johnnies so instantly recognisable wherever they went in Scotland. 'When I set off in the morning on my bike at Ayr,' says Guy Le Bihan, 'I'd have maybe thirty bunches hanging from the handlebars or over the carrier above the back wheel. So that would be about 350 or 360 onions altogether. Oh, it was very heavy!' It was that kind of weight that made the achievement of the young Jean Milin so remarkable when, as he modestly recalls, on one occasion he actually cycled all the way from Leith to Glasgow with his bicycle loaded with onions. 'Well, it was quite a flat road from Edinburgh to Glasgow,' he says. 'Oh, well, there weren't many hills. I set off very early in the morning.'

Yet in the earlier years of the twentieth century it was not the loaded bicycle but a wooden baton or pole carried over the shoulder that identified the Onion Johnny at work. 'You carried only one baton. That was enough!', says Jean Milin of his early days working as a teenage Johnny in Leith in the 1930s. 'I don't know, but I think the weight of the onions we carried for selling was about 25 or 30 kilogrammes – about 50 to 60 pounds. But we didn't go very far away with that load! . . . Of course, the weight was heaviest at the beginning of the day. Then, well, once you sold some it was lighter after that. Of course, when we were tired we used to put the baton on to the other shoulder to carry it. But the first eight days I was selling the onions my shoulder was sore, *oh, là, là*! As sailors say, I had a list to port!' Although the baton was being replaced by the 1930s by the bicycle, nonetheless as late as the early 1950s Jean-Marie Tanguy recalls that he used a baton on his selling rounds in Dundee.

Another earlier form of transport for the onions the Johnnies sold was a small handcart or *charrette*, and Jean

Saout and Jean Milin both recall pushing one through the streets of Glasgow or Leith respectively. But just as the bicycle gradually replaced the handcart and the baton, so the bicycle, if not replaced, was at least beginning to be supplemented in the later 1930s by the van. Vans, use of which by the Johnnies became much more widespread after the 1939–45 War, were employed as mobile depots from which the Johnnies, lifting out their loaded bikes once that day's destination was reached, could pedal their rounds and return to the van again for fresh supplies if needed. Other forms of transporting the onions are also mentioned by these veteran Johnnies. Anna Gourlet, when she began as an Onion 'Jenny' at Leith at the age of 13 or so in the early 1930s and before she acquired a bicycle, at first simply carried strings or bunches of onions in her hands. There are references also to the use of motor cycles, one of them with a sidecar which Jean-Marie Tanguy's father drove on his rounds at Dundee before the Second World War: 'But if there was rain or snow it was no good. Everything got soaked.' Tramcars and trains are also mentioned by several of the Johnnies as among the means they used for transporting their bicycles loaded with onions.

The distances or areas these Onion Johnnies covered from their bases in the cities and towns of Scotland may strike many readers as surprising, not to say astonishing. Although each company or family group of Johnnies was based in a particular city or town, the Johnnies did not confine themselves to making their rounds there. 'Glasgow was a big city,' Claude Quimerch rightly recalls. 'When we started in 1950 the population there was about a million. But, you see, there weren't enough customers for us in Glasgow! In Gorbals, for example, we weren't able to sell our onions. The people there'd got no money. I mean, Gorbals had many very poor people. And there was quite a lot of unemployment there. We needed to go where there was money. And then in Glasgow there were shops, vegetable shops, all around. So we had to go out more to the suburbs of Glasgow where people were better off, and then outside the city itself and away to other towns and places. There was much more money in places like Milngavie, Bearsden, Clarkston.' Thus Claude Quimerch, an employee or *ouvrier*, and something of a specialist as a van driver, in the company of Johnnies of which Jean Saout was a boss or *patron*, also found himself selling the company's onions in, for example, Balfron, Dumbarton, Balloch, Alexandria, Wemyss Bay, Gourock, Greenock, Johnstone, Kilbarchan, Paisley, Thornliebank, East Kilbride, Kilmarnock, Saltcoats, Largs, Muirkirk, Motherwell, Carluke, Lanark, Dumfries, Stranraer, Lochgilphead, Inveraray, Ardrishaig, Tarbert, Campbeltown, Machrihanish, and Oban, and even across the Border in Carlisle. Jean-Marie Tanguy, from the base of his father's company in Dundee, journeyed to sell its onions at Forfar, Brechin, Montrose, Laurencekirk, Kirriemuir, St Andrews, Crieff (where the Hydro was a particularly important customer), Comrie, and Perth. Jean Saout was unable to return home to St Pol de Léon to attend the funeral of his aged father in Brittany because of the lack of transport from Arran, where he was selling his onions at the time. Even as a young boy based in Glasgow he had accompanied his father to sell onions at Rothesay and Dunoon, and in later years he himself with his loaded bike went down the Clyde on the train to Greenock and Gourock, and also journeyed (with his bike, it seems, transported in his van) as far north as Fort William. The notes kept in his pocket diary in the autumn of 1977 by Guy Le Bihan provide further illustrations of distances covered and numbers and weight of onions sold in the course of a Johnny's daily work.[2]

'Well, we Onion Johnnies were always working. It was a hard life,' Jean Milin states. Since at least on some days considerable distances, some of them uphill, as, for example from Leith to Fairmilehead on the southern outskirts of Edinburgh, had to be covered with heavily laden bicycles,

Johnnies often had to set off early in the morning from their base if they were to find customers at home before they left for their places of work. At the other end of the day, as Guy Le Bihan puts it, 'It was a matter of pride almost for the Onion Johnnies not to return [to their base] with unsold onions!' Consequently, Johnnies' working hours were often very long. 'Well, you used to start sometimes at five o'clock in the morning,' Yves Rolland recalls of his years as a rank-and-file Johnny or *ouvrier* in Leith in the 1950s. 'And there was no finishing time. You had so many strings to sell in a day – and you had to sell them. I've seen myself when I was 14½, well, maybe I was 15½ . . . and I was in Musselburgh to sell onions. I went from Leith at five o'clock in the morning. And I came back again that day round about half past-ten at night. That wasn't a normal day's work. It depended how lucky you were. But normally it was round about seven or eight o'clock at night we used to finish. Most days the leaving time from the shop or the base was from about six, half-past six in the morning.' For the Johnnies there was no five-day week: Saturdays, at least till midday or mid-afternoon, were also working days, and on Sundays, although no onions were sold, there were almost always two or three hours that had to be devoted to stringing the onions or to gathering rushes from the fields for stringing them.

The system of payment of the Johnnies was distinctive, though it perhaps bore some resemblance to the payment of Scots farm workers in the nineteenth century at the end of their six months' engagements.[3] 'As for pay or wages, when I was a boy in Glasgow I got nothing,' Jean Saout recalls of his early years as a Johnny in that city in the 1920s. 'It was the boss who took the money. I passed all the money I got from selling the onions to my boss. My papa was a boss, too, but I never received money from him. At times I had nothing at all. I had perhaps only 6d. per month in those days. And, oh, 'a penny for myself' from customers! . . . But I never got a pay, a salary, in those days.' He was aged 26, he says, and had been working by then as a Johnny in Glasgow for almost two decades before he was able to retain some of his own pay. If the system of payment was difficult enough for Jean Saout as the son of a boss or *patron*, it was even worse for a rank-and-file Johnny or *ouvrier* such as Claude Quimerch. He was already married with one child when he became a Johnny in Glasgow in 1949–50, and he and his wife had their second daughter two or three years after that. Yet for the first four years he was a Johnny, Claude Quimerch was paid none of his wages until the end of the onion-selling season. 'So my wife had to live for six or seven months without any pay coming in . . . How she managed during those months for those four years is a mystery. We certainly didn't have plenty money! It was very hard, very, very hard. My wife didn't have a job because she had the girls to look after.' How precisely Madame Qimerch did manage at home in Santec she recounts below in an informative and eloquent addition to her husband's recollections. Many, perhaps most, other wives of Johnnies who were *ouvriers* must have suffered similar hardships.

The system of payment of the rank-and-file Johnnies and their long working hours might perhaps have been expected to provide some fertile ground for the growth among them of trade unionism. But the testimony of the five veterans below who mention that subject is unanimous: the Johnnies never had a union. No doubt its absence was a result of their working in relatively small groups, of the fact that the *patrons* or bosses not only worked beside the rank-and-file Johnnies or *ouvriers* but also lived in the same premises as them, and that in some cases, such as those of Anna Gourlet and François Perron, as well as of Guy Le Bihan, the business employed only or mainly members of one family.

Between the Onion Johnnies who came to Scotland each year for about a century and a half as seasonal immigrant workers and the Irish agricultural workers who came also each year during a rather longer era to work there on the hay, grain or potato harvests, there were perhaps some similarities. Both groups were Catholic (or, in the case of the Irish, predominantly so), some or many in each group spoke their respective native Celtic language, and members of both groups tended to keep (or, in the case of the Irish, generally housed in farm bothies, to be kept) separate from the local Scots population. (That is not at all to say, of course, that the Johnnies, any more or less than seasonal immigrant Irish workers, made no friends among Scots people: most of the nine veterans below give examples of friendships they formed and of hospitality they received.) After their season of work in Scotland, members of both groups returned home to work on their families' small farms or as labourers on others' farms, or, in the case of many of the Johnnies, in vegetable factories around Roscoff and St Pol de Léon or sometimes sugar beet farms in other areas of France. But if there were some ostensible similarities, there were also obvious differences between the two groups. One difference lay in the far greater numbers of Irish seasonal immigrant workers in Scotland compared with the relatively quite small numbers of Johnnies who worked there each year between July or August and the end of the selling season, usually at Christmas or early January. Moreover, unlike the Johnnies, who confined themselves to selling onions, many of the Irish found employment outside agriculture in a wide range of other industries and occupations. Moreover, while many Irish workers came eventually to settle permanently in Scotland in the nineteenth and twentieth centuries, very few Johnnies indeed appear to have done so. Only one or two cases of marriage between a Johnny and a Scots girl are recalled by the veterans below.[4] If the Irish figure large in the history of Scotland in the past two centuries, the Johnnies as a very small group are much more elusive. They do not appear in the decennial censuses, and as already indicated they seem rarely, unlike the Irish seasonal workers, to have attracted the attention of the newspapers.

That is why what these nine veterans have to say below about their working lives in Scotland forms a virtually unique record. Among the many other aspects of their lives that they touch on are their schooling (which for all of them except Claude Quimerch ended between the ages of eleven and fourteen), learning to speak English, competition between different companies of Johnnies, customers, varying techniques of selling onions, religious observance, leisure activities, contacts with home and family during the onion-selling season, credit-giving, conscript service in the French army or navy, camaraderie among the Johnnies, the frequency of their onion selling rounds, clothing worn, occasional catcalling by members of the local populace, vegetables other than onions that were sold, holidays, and reasons for the decline in the number of Onion Johnnies in Scotland from about the 1960s onwards.

On that last aspect, Yves Rolland comments: 'The people were too old. And there were no young ones taking their places. The young ones don't want to work as we did. Younger people didn't want to work the long hours that the Onion Johnnies worked. It wasn't anything to do with the Common Market or changes in the law. And younger people were finding work in factories and things like that at home in Brittany or elsewhere in France . . . So from, I would say, about 1985 I was the only Onion Johnny here. By then all the other Onion Johnnies had retired or weren't coming back to Scotland. Most of them were retiring age, you know, and they didn't sort of like coming still and doing the work. That was a big change, because Onion Johnnies had been coming to Scotland for about 150 years.' Guy Le Bihan expresses a somewhat different view of the reasons for the decline in the number of Onion Johnnies in Scotland. 'It wasn't that there was more employment around Roscoff and Santec and St Pol

de Léon by the time sons were growing up so that they didn't
need to become Onion Johnnies. It wasn't that. But there was
a big change for young people at home in Brittany and
everywhere. There was a new generation. I don't think it
was that young people were lazy. It was a difference in the
generations. Well, the young people remained at school or
college until they were 20 or more. I and other Onion
Johnnies had left school when we were fourteen or younger.
So after the young people left school they got a job of some
kind at home in Brittany. My wife and I, for instance, have
two sons and a daughter. The girl's teaching now in St Malo.
Her husband is in electronics. Our oldest son is manager in
the Crédit Agricole bank in Paimpol, and our other boy is an
engineer in Rennes. So they certainly wouldn't be interested
in giving up those jobs and going to sell onions in Scotland.
Young people have a higher level of education than we and
the older Johnnies – Ingan Johnnies, as we were called in
Scotland – ever had and there was more variety of employment for them than there was for us, their parents or grandparents. It wasn't because they were lazy they didn't become
Onion Johnnies, because they have had to work hard to
become teachers and managers and engineers and so on. But
it was a different world for them from what it was for us
older ones. So I think that was the main reason for the decline
in the number of Onion Johnnies in Ayrshire, in Scotland,
and in Britain as a whole.'

In transcribing and editing these recollections, every effort
has been made to preserve the actual spoken words of the
nine veteran Johnnies. Four of them spoke wholly or mainly
in French, one partly in French and partly in English, and the
other four in English. (There were also some occasional
interjections in Breton.) Each veteran checked and approved
the edited version of his or her verbatim transcript. As part of
the policy of the Scottish Working People's History Trust to

make its work as generally available and accessible as possible, the audio tapes and a copy of each verbatim transcript will be deposited by the Trust in due course in the School of Scottish Studies at Edinburgh University, and if possible in the Musée des Johnnies at Roscoff, and a copy of any relevant tape and transcript will likewise be deposited in appropriate local public repositories in Scotland.

The Scottish Working People's History Trust is glad to acknowledge the indispensable help it has received from many people and organisations in carrying out this oral history project, the first it has undertaken where interviews were carried out outside Scotland itself. To the nine veteran Onion Johnnies below warm thanks are due for their co-operation and helpfulness in recalling their experiences. The spouses and families of the Johnnies were no less helpful and hospitable. Particular thanks are also due to Monsieur Paul Caroff of Roscoff, himself a former Onion Johnny who worked in England, for finding for the Trust the eight surviving Johnnies in Brittany who had worked in Scotland and for accompanying me to most of the interviews with them. Staff of the French Consulate General in Edinburgh, Madame Véronique Penot of the Musée des Johnnies at Roscoff, and Monsieur Joseph Seite, mayor of Roscoff, provided helpful information. Frédéric Simon and Jérome Blanchard, Breton students in Edinburgh, rendered invaluable assistance in checking transcriptions of the interviews. Among librarians, archivists and curators in Scotland who either provided or at least tried to find references to Onion Johnnies in their localities, thanks are due to Dorothy Kidd, Scottish Life Archive, National Museums of Scotland, Fiona Myles and Ian Nelson and their colleagues in the Scottish and Edinburgh departments of Edinburgh Public Libraries, Sheila Millar, Midlothian, Veronica Wallace, East Lothian, M. Sybil Cavanagh, West Lothian, William Millan, Bennie Museum, Bathgate, Chris Neale, Dunfermline, Janet Klak, Kirkcaldy,

Introduction

Eileen Moran, Dundee, Rosalyn J. Rennie and Morag Allan, Aberdeen, Alistair Campbell, Elgin, Enda Ryan, The Mitchell Library, Glasgow, Jeanette Castle, Ayr, Mrs Alison Farrer, Ardrossan, Graham Hopner, Dumbarton, Jacqueline Ritchie, Paisley, John McLeish, East Kilbride, Mrs Couperwhite, Greenock, Mrs Christine Miller, Kirkintilloch, Irene McIntyre, Falkirk, and Gillian McNay and Helen Darling, Selkirk. The Trust is especially grateful to Dr John and Mrs Val Tuckwell of Tuckwell Press for their indispensable support of its work. Without the willingness of my wife Sandra to transport me from one end of Brittany to the other and back again, interviewing the Johnnies would have been much more difficult. Whatever shortcomings may be found in the completed work are to be blamed on me alone.

Ian MacDougall,
Secretary and Research Worker,
The Scottish Working People's History Trust.

JEAN SAOUT

I was only eight years old when I first came to Scotland – to Glasgow – to sell onions. That was in 1921. I was born at Ker André, St Pol de Léon, in Brittany on the 6th of February 1913, just before the First World War. I came to Scotland that first time with my father and on his passport.

My father was an Onion Johnny. He worked in Scotland, in Glasgow. But he had worked in England, too, though I don't know where. He always worked several months every year as an Onion Johnny in Britain but during the rest of every year he worked in Brittany as a small tenant farmer. He had first gone as an Onion Johnny to Britain when he was very, very young – perhaps at the age of 10 or 11. My father died when he was 86. I'm not sure but I think that was about 1961. So he must have been born in the 1870s and first went as an Onion Johnny to Britain in the 1880s. What I remember is that I was working as an Onion Johnny in Arran when my father died, so I couldn't go to his funeral. My wife sent me a telegram on Arran, saying my father had died. There were no aeroplanes from Arran, and the ferry boat had already sailed. My wife sent me another telegram: 'Father buried'. So there was no point then in going home.

My father had been called up to the French army in the 1914–18 War. But after some time he was demobilised. A law came out that said if a soldier had five children he could leave the army and go home. Well, my father by then had five children and he had married for the third time. By his first marriage he had two daughters, my half-sisters. By his second marriage he had three children, of whom I was one. By his third marriage during the 1914–18 War he had five children. So there were ten of us children altogether by my father's three marriages: five boys, including me, and five girls. What a life for my father. But things were like that at that time. He didn't have much luck. At any rate, he was too old to fight in the 1939–45 War.

I never knew my mother. She had died when I was only three months old in 1913. And then, as I say, my father was called up when the 1914–18 War began. So I was put into an orphanage during the War and I was in it for five years. It was during that time my father remarried for the third time. Then my father and my stepmother came to fetch me from the orphanage. We lived there at Ker André, near St Pol de Léon.

When I began at school you had to walk to St Pol every morning. It was three kilometres' walk to the school, and three kilometres back home. We wore wooden sabots or clogs. We were very poor as a family.

I attended the secular or state school at St Pol at first. The priest didn't want me to remain at that school. He got me to leave and I went to the church school then. We didn't have the money at home to pay the fees but the priest paid them for us. Years later, when I was an Onion Johnny in Scotland, one of my customers said to me, 'Oh, Jean, Jean, you are a very clever boy.' I said, 'Oh, no, no, no, I don't think so. I didn't know my mother, I didn't know my mother. I've never been in school long enough. I can't read English or write it.' Well, I left school at St Pol when I was about twelve. But by then I had already been working in Glasgow for three summers, selling onions.

That first time when I was only eight years old I went with my father to Glasgow to sell onions and I went on his passport it was in 1921. I just said, 'I'm going with papa to Britain.' At that time we had three months' holiday in the summer from school at St Pol. So I worked in Glagow with my father during those three months. Then I went back to school again in St Pol. So I did that for three seasons, or at least three summers.

That first time I went to Glasgow in 1921 we set off from St Pol on the 25th of July. In those days the onions were ready sooner than they are nowadays. Now they are a bit later. That's because it used to be warmer in those days. So we went earlier. Then, too, the onions weren't as dry as they are now. So normally when I was young the Onion Johnnies went to Britain in the month of July to begin the season of selling the onions. The Pardon – a Breton religious festival – took place on the 15th or 16th of July. So the Johnnies set off from home about ten days later. The first three seasons I went to Glasgow I went, as I say, for three months – July until September, when I had to go back to school at St Pol.

My impressions of Glasgow when I first went there with my father to sell onions were, well, when I went to the houses I rang the bell or knocked on the door. Someone would open the door and you'd say, 'You want some onions today, please?' 'Oh, not today, thank you.' Then they would close the door. The next door after was the same. I would climb three, four, five storeys with a baton hanging with onions on my shoulder. Tired, oh, tired! I certainly was after that.

For us young boys a baton would have almost 25 or 30 kilogrammes of onions on it – about 60 lbs. Oh! Tired, did you say? But you had to get on with it, even if you were only eight or nine years old as I was. And you went up and down the stairs with the onions. Sometimes when you were going down the stairs again a door would open: 'How much is your onions?' At first I didn't know what to say, I didn't speak a word of English. Afterwards when you went back to the shop, our base, I'd say to the other Onion Johnnies: 'A lady asked me, "How much?" What does that mean?' 'That means how much – *Combien c'est?*' So the next day I knew.

Then the onions cost 1s.3d. for a little bunch or string. A full bunch – two strings – was 2s.6d. But of course I didn't know at first what 1s.3d. was. You said to the customer, 'One and three – 1s.3d. Yes – and a penny for myself, please. And the big bunch – 2s.6d., *deux six*, 2s.6d.' A big bunch was a *grande botte*. Two strings made one bunch. There were about 11 onions then in a string and about 22 in a bunch. Years ago it was different. Then you had three strings of onions in a bunch.

When you made a bunch of onions you started it with the big onions and after that the small onions, then big ones again. That made the bunch prettier, more attractive for commercial reasons. So big ones first then smaller ones, then again bigger ones.

Each Onion Johnny sold about two hundredweight of onions every day. In a string there was about 3½ lbs of onions and about 7lbs in a bunch. Sometimes someone – a customer – would say, 'Oh, I'll give you a shilling for your onions.' You'd say, 'No, I can't. I must give the money to the boss.' I had to do that. If you had no' the right amount of money to give the boss, well . . . I sold so many bunches, so I had so much money to give to the boss. He counted your money every night, you see.

Sometimes, as I say, I'd ask a customer for a penny for myself. Sometimes someone would say, 'I don't like onions. But wait a minute.' He'd give me a sixpence then: 'Well, it's for you, not for the boss.'

When I went first to Glasgow when I was eight years old we lived in a shop in Kingston Street, near the Central Station and near the river Clyde. You used to hear all day, oh, all day, bbbbbrrrrhhhhh, bbbbbrrrrrhhhhh – hammering and banging of metal as ships were being built on the river. It was a big shop. You slept there, too. My father and I and all the Onion Johnnies slept there. There were perhaps eight or nine Johnnies and perhaps about six bosses, too – *patrons*. It was a company. My father was one of the bosses. Another boss was Monsieur Gallou and there were two named Chapalain, and another two named Peter and Franc.

We had trunks to keep our clothes and things in. But there weren't any beds. We slept on straw and we had blankets to cover ourselves with. It was only on Sundays we shook up the straw with a pitchfork. And then we carried on sleeping on it. You had pillows, too. They were filled with hay. Sometimes you had bits of straw that marked your face when you slept. But you slept well, you slept well.

I remember there was an old boss. He was a bit mixed up at times. Sometimes he would say about two o'clock in the morning, 'No one is going to get up here. The postman has long since passed.' Then his son would say, 'Oh, go and be quiet. The postman's still asleep. It's only two o'clock in the morning.' Then in the morning the old man would walk on our feet to waken us.

When you got up in the morning, well, you just had a cup o' tea. Then you left the shop with your baton of onions on your shoulder and you had a little two-wheeled handcart. There were four of us with the cart. I was in the shafts of the cart and the others pulled it along with ropes in front. You covered four or five kilometres in the morning but you had to go back with the cart to the shop in the evening. That was always my job in the second year I was at Glasgow. I was nine years old by then. At the age of eight, nine, ten – I did three summers like that before I began work full-time as an Onion Johnny.

As I say, on your baton on your shoulder you had 25 or 30 kilos – about 60 lbs – of onions. And when you had sold them you went back to the little cart to fetch more for sale. The cart held about 500 or 600 kilos of onions. As we were young boys we had fewer onions to sell among the four of us.

Sometimes you put the wheels of the cart into the tramlines and ran along with it more quickly. Once I had turned the cart too abruptly and the tail end caught the lamp of a motor car and broke the lamp.

I remember once we had passed the bridge over the Clyde near Central Station. We were lost then the whole evening. We were afraid and we were hungry. Each of us took a turnip to eat from a field. Then the police found us. We couldn't speak English at that time. But I had a paper in my pocket which I showed to the police. It said, 'We stay in Kingston Street', and it showed the police we were lost. The police just said, 'Oh, la, la. Seventh street on your left, and turn right and straight on after that.' When you knew what street it was you found the shop immediately. But at that time you didn't know how to ask the way. That was why we were afraid.

Well, I worked for three summers like that with the little cart. Then one day I took the last three bunches of onions from the cart and went to sell them. When I came back to the cart the other three boys had gone. I looked for them but they had gone away back to the shop in a tramcar. So I went back there too in a tramcar. The other three boys were in the shop selecting and stringing onions. After that I said, 'I'm not going back again with them, I'm not going back with them any more. Buy me a bike'. Well, the bike when I got it didn't have any pedals! So much the worse for my onions! But I didn't go back again with those other three boys.

When I first sold onions in Glasgow I was the youngest. I was eight. The other boys were perhaps 11, 12, 13, or 14 years old. But I was tall for my age as a boy. Now as an old man I'm not so tall, because I've lost my hair!

I always worked then with my father in Glasgow. But he wasn't there all the time to keep an eye on me, because he went off to sell onions in places like Rothesay and Dunoon. I went twice there with him as a young boy but otherwise I was always at work in Glasgow.

I left school in St Pol de Léon when I was about 11 or 12. So after working for three summers selling onions in Glasgow while I was still at school, I began to work the whole onion-selling season in Glasgow, from July until about Christmas. When I went back home then to St Pol I worked the other months of the year *chez* Henri. Henri was a vegetable merchant. I was employed by him every year as an *emballeur*, a packer. At Henri's I worked with cauliflowers, onions, artichokes, carrots, shallots, garlic – all sorts of vegetables. So for those months every year from when I was 13 years old I worked *chez* Henri at St Pol. I worked there until Henri died. In fact, I worked there for 42 years. It was *chez* Henri – Glasgow – *chez* Henri – Glasgow, for 42 years. When the season came for going again to Britain, to Glasgow, I said, 'No, I'm going to Britain.' But as soon as I came back from Glasgow at the end of every season I went back again to work *chez* Henri at St Pol. That's how it was.

After the 1914–18 War, when I began as a boy selling onions in Glasgow, there were three or four big companies of Onion Johnnies there. In our company, as I've said, there were about 14 or 15: six *patrons* or bosses and about eight or nine *ouvriers* or ordinary Johnnies. But there were some small companies of Johnnies, too, of maybe only three or four men. Altogether there were perhaps round about 40 Johnnies working in Glasgow then.

There was a lot of competition between the companies after the 1914–18 War. In fact, there were too many Johnnies there then. There were two, three, even four Johnnies who went along the same streets selling onions. So a customer would say, 'You are a nuisance! There should be a maid here to open the door to you all!' The Johnnies went to the same customers or clients. So that created bother. There was no agreement between the companies for each to sell their onions only in some particular area of Glasgow. It wasn't that some agreed to sell them south of the River Clyde there and others to the north of the river. Oh, no, there was nothing like that. It was all mixed up, all mixed up. Oh, there was a lot of competition. But there weren't quarrels between the companies.

Jean Saout

Customers were loyal. You had your regular customers. When Johnnies from other companies came to them, 'Oh, yes, but they sell onions that are too dear.' 'How much do you sell them for? They would say, 'A shillin', one shillin'.' 'Oh, no. I'll buy them from the same man who always comes here. He's been coming since a long time ago. Oh, no, I don't change.' And they would say, 'Oh, you are not the man who came here before. No. I know my friend who comes here. His mother is dead.' That was me!

Sometimes you could sell twenty bunches of onions in an hour. Other times you could go for an hour without selling a single bunch. It was a matter of luck. Some cities were better than others. When you laughed a little you sold the onions more easily than when you were sad! And then, of course, sometimes when you rang the bell of a house a big dog would come: 'Ggggrrrr . . . ggggrrrr.' You went on then up to the next landing if it was a tenement house!

I don't know why but often when I stopped at houses numbered 13 and 14 it brought me good luck. I often sold onions at those numbers. The street was arranged in odd and even numbers. Well, I almost always stopped, crossed the road and it was rare for me not to sell any. I don't know what it was but those numbers 13 and 14 were lucky doors.

Sometimes, of course, customers grew their own onions, too. Once years ago I had a customer in Glasgow at Knightswood. Knightswood wasn't old then. In fact, I saw it being built. There weren't any houses at first, Knightswood was just a farm. I remember one day when I went to my customer's place there and opened the gate there was a little garden that was full of onions. But I saw they were all leaning over. They were worm-eaten. Well, my customer said to me, 'Oh, Jean, excuse me. Got plenty onions in the garden this year.' 'Ah,' I said, 'but your onions is no' good.' 'Why? Don't say that to my husband!' 'Well,' I said, 'they're all full of grubs.' 'Oh, it's not true.' 'Come and see,' I said. So I lifted the head of an onion and showed her how it was all eaten away. It was covered in white grubs. 'Oh, I'm going to let my husband see that when he comes back this evening.' Well, I called on customers every fortnight. The next time I went there there were no heads on the onions. The whole lot had been thrown in the dustbin!

Then I had some customers who would say to me, 'John, I like your onions. But we have no money.' 'Well,' I said, 'I trust you, I trust you. You pay next time. I trust you.' Yes, I had some good customers. But then I had some others that weren't like that. I would go to them on a Saturday. I had given one woman credit like that, too. And I saw the woman at the window in her kitchen. I rang the bell and knocked at the door. But she didn't open it. In fact, she didn't come to the door, because she owed me some money. 'Ah,' I said, 'that's it finished now. You'll have no more credit from me.'

A mate, a *copain*, of mine named Chapalain busied himself selling onions to the hotels in Glasgow. I sold onions and shallots also to hotels there, and to restaurants as well. I sold a lot in hotels. Chapalain sold a lot of garlic, too, every Monday to the Italians in Glasgow. Though we sold a lot of garlic in Scotland, the Scots themselves didn't like garlic. When I was cooking a meal in the shop in Kingston Street and there were women walking along the pavement when the door was open, they'd say, 'Oh, what a smell!' But it was a good smell, the smell they got from the garlic. Perhaps I have a good memory because I ate a lot of garlic!

Each day all the onions we took out to sell had to be sold. All of them had to be sold. Onions weren't to be taken back to the shop. That was because every Johnny had to give his account. In the early days when I worked in Glasgow, those of us who were just boys had fewer onions to sell. In my case I didn't know how to speak English then.

The hours of work sometimes began at 6.30 or 7 o'clock in the morning. It depended on where you were going to sell the onions. Sometimes it would be four or five kilometres away from the shop in Kingston Street. You began to knock on doors at 9 o'clock. You were working at times from 9 o'clock in the morning until 9 o'clock at night. As I've said, all the onions had to be sold.

So you got up in the morning about 6 o'clock or 5.30 to get your bike loaded up with onions. You took a cup o' tea in the morning and some bread. But you didn't eat anything during the day, not at all. You sold the onions the whole time. The Johnnies who worked in the shop stringing the onions they ate at midday, and sometimes they had a snack at 4 o'clock in the afternoon. But everybody finished work at 9 o'clock at night.

On Saturdays we worked normally just like on the other days, except that we finished at midday selling the onions and then after that we worked in the shop. Saturday was the best day for us selling the onions because people were at home and they had their pay. On Sundays we worked only in the mornings. We didn't sell any onions on Sundays, not one. What we did was stringing onions in the shop.

As for pay or wages, when I was a boy in Glasgow I got nothing. It was the boss who took the money. I passed all the money I got from selling the onions to my boss. My papa was a boss, too, but I never received money from him. At times I had nothing at all. I had perhaps only 6d. per month in those days. And, oh, 'a penny for myself' from customers! The old Johnnies when the work was finished, well, the pub opened at five o'clock, I think. You sat on the shafts of their little handcarts and looked for 6d. for chips for your supper and then you ate them. When at times you had a dozen coppers in your pocket you got some Italian ice cream. You got an ice cream cone. But I never got a pay, a salary, in those days. If you had enough money to buy one you bought a cake or something. You see, you sold onions but you had to account for them to the boss. You had to sell so many bunches. The money was put on the trunks and counted. If it was short, well . . . You had to watch out the next time. Oh, it was a hard life. All the bosses passed all your money to your mother. But just before the 1939–45 War, when I was 26, I asked my stepmother to let me keep some of the money also. That was in 1938. I had got 11,000 francs during that season. Then in 1939 I lost 3,000 francs because we had to leave Glasgow and go home to fight in the war.

As I say, the Onion Johnnies left Brittany normally toward the end of July for Britain. After my first three years at Glasgow as a boy aged eight to ten, when I came back home again at the end of the school summer holidays, I stayed on at Glasgow selling the onions until November or December every year. We always came back for Christmas. Some Johnnies stayed on in Britain longer than that – some of them for nine months – but me, no. I never stayed there till January or February. In December I was back home at St Pol de Léon. I was always back home for Christmas – and to work with the vegetables *chez* Henri.

Some Johnnies who came home in the winter couldn't find work in Brittany – so they went back again to Britain. Unemployment could be bad at times at home. The cold weather could stop the growth of the cauliflowers. So the working year wasn't always a regular routine, it wasn't always a simple matter. It depended on finding employment at home in Brittany.

As for the onions we sold in Britain, well, I had good customers in Scotland because I gave them good onions. They knew that. The onions came from Plouescat and from Roscoff. People always speak about the *oignons rosés,* the pink onions of Roscoff. But they were onions from Plouescat, too. Those were pink onions as well. They arrived in the Clyde at Glasgow by boat from Brittany. Cargoes of onions arrived there perhaps two or three times during the selling season. The boat went also to Aberdeen or Dundee or Leith, too. Our shop in Glasgow in Kingston Street was beside Kingston dock. A big company of Onion Johnnies like ours in Glasgow took perhaps 50 tons of onions. Our company, when I was young, used to sell during the season about 30 or 40 tons of onions. That's why the shop was there. A shop was necessary for storing the onions in. The owner of the shop was a Mr Pickard. He owned whole streets in Glasgow. He himself lived at Bearsden. Oh, he was a millionaire, Mr Pickard.[5]

The onions were sold by the Johnnies when I was a boy in Glasgow from a baton – a pole over their shoulder, from which strings and bunches of onions hung – and from the *charrette*, the little handcart. In those days Onion Johnnies didn't have bikes. I got a bike when I was a bit older, as I say, but it had no pedals. It was just a means of being able to push the onions along more easily. Then the Onion Johnnies could use the tramway in Glasgow, too, to get about with their onions.

The bikes I had were always Scots bikes. So I always kept to the left of the road! But I never had a French bike in Glasgow, always Scots. They were always old bikes. You put strings or a net around the wheels to prevent onions going between the spokes. Otherwise it was dangerous. But I never suffered any accidents on the bike, never. The bike, when it was loaded up with onions was not heavy to pedal on a flat surface, but on hills you got off and walked, oh, là là! And when you went downhill you went gently, gently, using your brakes. But I never suffered any accidents on the bike.

I never suffered from homesickness when I worked in Glasgow. There I went off to work just the same as I did at home in Brittany.

Sometimes on a Saturday afternoon I went to the football match, when there was a big match on, an international, or Celtic or Rangers. I supported Celtic and Rangers! They said Celtic were Catholic and Rangers Protestant, but it was all the same to me. In the government there are Protestants and

Catholics or Communists or merchants – the lot. To me it's all the same! So sometimes it was Celtic and Rangers, sometimes an international match at Hampden Park. But it was only sometimes I went to the match, because Saturday was a working day, too. That was the day people got their pay.

On Sundays I didn't go often to the mass in Glasgow – now I don't go at all! At home in St Pol de Léon I was obliged to go to mass every Sunday with my father. People after mass would speak about the market and how much you'd paid for artichokes, how much you paid for this and that – well, they were peasants. That was life at home in Brittany. Well, I'm going to say something that you may think isn't true. But it is true. I went once to a priest's house – a presbytery – in Glasgow to sell onions. The priest said to me, 'You're French. Do you go to church?' I said, 'Church?' He said to me, 'Well, don't come here if you don't go to church every day.' I said, 'I come here when I'm working'. He said, 'But on a Sunday?' I said, 'On Sunday I go sometimes.' 'Sometimes? What church do you go to?' 'Well,' I says, 'St Andrew's, near Central Station.' 'Well,' the priest said, 'go and sell your onions elsewhere. I don't want them.' I said, 'Merci. Thank you very much all the same.' And there was a Protestant minister, who was married with three children. This minister said to me, 'You are Catholic or Protestant?' 'Well,' I said, 'I'm a Catholic, yes.' He said, 'You go to church sometimes, I see. Very good. How much is your onions?' '1s.3d. and 2s.6d. for the big bunch.' 'Oh, well,' he said, 'give me four bunches and three bunches for my friend.' I said to myself, 'Oh, well, I must go to his church sometime. He bought some onions.' But the priest he turned me away although he was a Catholic like me.

And then on Sundays in Glasgow I did the cooking in the shop. There were perhaps a dozen or fourteen Onion Johnnies in the company. You bought a leg of mutton. Well, while the others were stringing the onions in the shop on Sundays I did the cooking in the kitchen. I made some holes in the gigot of mutton. In the holes I put some cloves of garlic. That was when women passing along the pavement in front of the shop would say when our door was open, 'Oh, what a smell!' I always ate garlic with *bifteck*, frying steak. When you came back in the evening after selling the onions you had *bifteck* to eat. Every Johnny in our company in Glasgow had his pound of *bifteck* every day. When you got back to the shop in the evening you cooked your *bifteck* and ate it. Nowadays sometimes when my wife cooks steak I'll say to her, 'Oh, it's overdone, it's overdone.' When it's like that it's over-cooked and it's not good. But also in the evenings when you came back to the shop sometimes you had soup and *pot-au-feu* - stew. Sometimes there was thick fat on the pot and you had to reheat it.

During the day customers would sometimes ask you, 'John, you want a cup o' tea?' I'd say, 'Oh, no – no time, no time.' 'Well, I'll give you a piece of bread.' Butter was spread on the bread and then some jam on the top of it and then another slice of bread was added to it. In Glasgow that was a jammy piece. I was pleased. But every day customers would give you bread. They said, 'Well, come, come.' And you would say, 'Oh, no. No time, oh, no.' But after a time you got into the habit. You ate too much then.

On Sunday afternoons, well, you rested or slept if you wanted to. And on Sunday evenings you went to bed again.

In 1933 I had to go to France to do my military service in the army. I was born in 1913 and at the age of twenty you had to go to the army. In the army I had a *copain*, a mate, who didn't smoke and I didn't drink. I was 21 before I ever tasted wine. But I smoked when I was young. At midday everyone had his quarter litre of wine in the army. Then, I said to my mate, 'If you don't smoke I'll smoke your tobacco and you can drink my wine.' So it was arranged like that. Then he had two quarter litres of wine to drink and I had two packets of cigarettes.

Around the time I had done my army service and came back to sell onions in Glasgow about 1935, the straw on which the Johnnies had slept in Kingston Street had been replaced by beds. Well, we still slept in the shop there but from then we had beds to sleep in. By then, too, the baton and the little *charrette* or handcart for carrying the onions had gone and the Onion Johnnies had bikes that they loaded with onions.

Then in 1939 when I went back for the onion-selling season to Scotland a customer said to me one day, 'Oh, you've come again. But the war has been declared.' I didn't know. That was September. By then we'd been in Scotland about a month. But then, of course, I was obliged to go back to France to fight in the war. That was how, as I say, I lost 3,000 francs that year. My father remained there in Glasgow for a time because he was too old to serve in the war. So he stayed there for a time and so did the young lads, too. But then or a bit later on, when all the onions had been sold, all the Onion Johnnies came back to France.

When I was on the boat coming back then to France from, I think it was Portsmouth – you didn't know where you were – the captain said: 'Above all do not smoke! Because a match lit at sea can be seen from far off.' Well, a lot of Onion Johnnies went down below on the boat to have a cigarette. Even if there had been a submarine the Johnnies would still have wanted to have a puff. But the captain said, 'Above all do not smoke on board in time of war.' I think it was at Cherbourg that we disembarked then.

So then I was in the army. But I wasn't long in the war. The Germans invaded France. But I didn't become a prisoner of war. I ran away too quickly, I ran away too quickly! I went back home and I worked again at the vegetable merchant's, *chez* Henri. The Germans were stationed near where we lived at St Pol de Léon, just about 600 metres away. Sometimes they fired a big gun down on the beach nearby. You could hear the shells – zoooom! zooom! It fairly whistled. Well, the German occupation lasted four years.

During the war, in 1942, when I was 29 I got married. It was a difficult time. My wife and I had three children. My wife never worked outside our home after we were married. She never came to Scotland to work with me after the war. It was a difficult life for her bringing up the children when after the war I was away selling onions again in Scotland.

There was one Onion Johnny I remember who married a Scots girl. He married a lady at Ayr and he lived there. His wife didn't come to live in France. They remained at Ayr and their children, too. But there weren't any Scots girls who married Johnnies and came to live in Brittany. There were only one or two Johnnies who married Scots girls but I remember only that one who lived at Ayr. But he and his wife are dead now and their children went to America.

Well, after the war, I went back again to Glasgow to sell onions. I think that was in 1946 or 1947. I was a *patron*, a boss, then. But ours was the only company of Onion Johnnies in Glasgow after the 1939–45 War. There were only about a dozen Johnnies in our company then. And as the years passed it became smaller. Numbers ranged from five or six to three or four Johnnies. There had been about 40 Johnnies in Glasgow before the war. Another change was that we had a small van – *une petite camionette* - by then. Claude Quimerch was my van driver. Onion Johnnies hadn't had vans for carrying the onions when I was young before the war.

Our shop was still in Kingston Street in Glasgow after the war. In the shop we had beds in tiers, one on top of the other, like bunks. They were in three or four tiers. There was a big room for the onions, a separate room for sleeping in, and a little square place for doing the cooking in. There was a wc and a sink where you could wash. So there were four places there altogether. When after the war there were a dozen Johnnies living there it was a bit crowded. But we all passed an agreeable time there. We were all friendly, we were all *copains*, all mates. There were no quarrels – well, maybe with certain ones.

There was never a trade union of Onion Johnnies in Glasgow. There was an Association of Johnnies at home in Brittany but it wasn't a trade union.

As I said, I'd gone with my father a couple of times when I was a boy selling onions at Rothesay and Dunoon. Then after I got a bike I went selling onions at Inveraray, Lochgilphead, Ardrishaig, Tarbert, Campbeltown, Oban, Fort William. I went down the Clyde to Greenock and Gourock, too. In those days you went to Central Station in Glasgow with the bike loaded with onions and took the train. Then there was a boat, a ferry, which left every Monday and went to Campbeltown. And then afterward you took the boat to return to Glasgow. But after that I used to go to the isle of Arran with onions. I took the train from Central Station to Ardrossan and from Ardrossan I took the ferry to Brodick on Arran. I stayed on Arran the whole week then. It was a case in those days of a week working at Rothesay, a week on Arran, and a fortnight at Glasgow.

When I got off the boat at Brodick I used to sleep at Glen Rosa. When you got off at Brodick you turned to the right. It was a house at Glen Rosa, well, it was a little farm. Two old women and two men – they were brothers and sisters who weren't married – lived there.

At night on Arran you had to watch out for deer, oh, big deer, when you had your lamp on. When you left your bike at the edge of the road with the lamp on it wasn't good for the deer. Then they crossed the road – whew! As you went down the road they crossed – whoof! And then the deer fought each other, too. When there was a herd of females one male would challenge another male and then there was a fight! But Arran was fine, it was fine, very beautiful. From Brodick to Blackwater Foot I used to cross the island that way. I cycled all round Arran on my bike with onions – the whole island, all the farms also.

On Arran there were three or four farms where the people would say, 'Eh, there's somebody else wants onions, too.' I would say, 'Oh, no, it's too far for me to go there – too hilly, too hilly. Non, non, I lose my time.' They would say, 'No, no. I'm going to take them for you. I'm going to buy them for those other people. I'll pay you.' So they took the onions to send them on afterwards to the other people.

Sometimes the lady of a house would tell me that other people somewhere needed some onions. But I would say, 'Oh, it's too far. They are going to take maybe one bunch and for that perhaps I'll take three quarters of an hour or an hour to go there and come back.' It wasn't worth it for the sake of selling just a few of the onions.

When I was on Arran I was a bit like a baker on his rounds. I knew where to go. People said to me, 'The next time tell me when you're coming. I'll take twice as many.' But, as I say, I had good customers because I was giving them good onions.

After the 1939–45 War, of course, we had a van. Then you went to Campbeltown with the van. You slept in hotels, hotels that bought our onions from us. The hotels and us gained from each other. When Claude Quimerch was the van driver after the war we went with the van to Campbeltown and Fort William and so on. You put the onions in the van and then loaded the bikes with them. I did the rounds of the farms, only the farms, and my *copain*, my mate he did the towns, the little towns and villages. When I went to Campbeltown, well, we started at Inveraray. At Inveraray I put onions on my bike and I did the farms along the road and off the road. My mate he went as far as Ardrishaig on his bike loaded with onions. So we had the van then and the two bikes. But my mate didn't have much need for using a bike because he made use of the van. You worked along the whole road but you finished selling the onions at Fort William more or less, and then you went back to Glasgow.

Elsewhere in Scotland there were companies of Onion Johnnies at Dundee and Edinburgh. At Edinburgh there were the Tanguys and the Perrons. The Johnnies at Dundee used to come to Campbeltown and to Glasgow, too, to sell their onions. I never heard of any Johnnies selling onions in the Hebrides in places like Lewis or on Skye, or on Orkney or Shetland. They were too far away, I think.

Well, I never got rich selling onions, ah, no! I just made enough to live on and to drink a little glass of wine. But I never wanted to change my job, never. I never had any ambition to do any other job like being a seaman or working on the railways. It was the same when I was working the other months of the year with the vegetables at home in Brittany, *chez* Henri. After the 1939–45 War I was asked if I wouldn't like to stay in St Pol de Léon and work there. By then I'd worked for more than twenty years *chez* Henri. But I didn't change, I didn't want to.

Well, I gave up being an Onion Johnny in Glasgow in 1965. By then I was 52 years old. I had been an Onion Johnny off and on by then for over 40 years. By that time our company was the last company of Onion Johnnies in Glasgow and I was about the last of the Johnnies there. You see, the Johnnies who worked in Britain lost a lot of pension when they came to retire. Their work there didn't count for the full state pension.

But I carried on working at home in Brittany from the age of 52 until I was 65. I worked those years still with the vegetables – onions, garlic, cauliflowers. And then I worked, too, in some of the local farms belonging to *copains*, pals. So in 1978 I retired completely.

A few years before then, maybe about 1974, I went back to

Scotland on holiday, with my wife and my son and daughter-in-law. We crossed the Channel from Roscoff to Portsmouth. We were on Arran then we went to Glasgow. But I didn't know anybody by that time. Things had changed. I went to the farms where I used to sell onions – but everything had changed. I asked for the people I used to sell the onions to but they were gone, retired. It was their sons and daughters who were on the farms by that time and, oh, they didn't know me. Well, some of them did. It was sad. They asked me, 'Do you have any onions?' I said, 'No, I'm on holiday.' 'Ah, you've made a lot of money, is that it?' You just had to laugh.

Well, now I'm 86 and when I think back to all those years I was an Onion Johnny in Scotland I don't think of anything really. I'm just glad to open my eyes in the morning and have a quiet day! Then I go and do a little work in my garden and have a game of *boule*, French bowls, along the road from home at the Tahiti place.

The life of the Onion Johnnies was hard – and it was hard for their wives and families at home, too. But you had to live as best you could. I wouldn't like to begin all over again, though at least one doesn't sleep on straw any more! I don't regret having worked as an Onion Johnny at Glasgow. But it was a hard job, too hard.

JEAN MILIN

The first time I went to Leith to sell onions I was still at school. I had a friend the same age as me who said to me one day, 'Come on with me and sell onions in Britain.' *Voilà!* I was just twelve years old then.

I was born at Plouescat in Brittany, not far from where I live now and which is about 20 kilometres west of Roscoff, on the 9th of May 1917, during the First World War. My father was at Verdun in the French army when I was born. In fact, he came to our house for eight days' leave – but he stayed on for six weeks. He didn't want to go back again! The war was horrible.

My father was a small farmer at Plouescat. He had about five hectares – a dozen acres. So it was quite a small farm. We had two horses and four cows. My father grew onions on his farm but he never worked as an Onion Johnny. We used to go with onions with the horses from Plouescat to Brest, which was about 90 kilometres away, and to Landerneau, which was 28 kilometres. But he was a fisherman, too, at times because at Plouescat we were right beside the sea. So he worked on the farm and also did a little bit of fishing from time to time. He did the farming in the spring, the summer and the autumn and the fishing in the winter months.

My father was born about 1894. He had already done his conscript military service in the French army before the war. He was called up again to go to the war in, I think, 1914 or 1915. He was at the battle of Verdun in 1916 and, as I say, was there in 1917 when I was born. He died when he was 80, about 1974.

Jean Milin

My grandfather Milin, who lived until he was 93, he was a farmer, too.

My mother was the daughter of a small farmer as well. She had four sisters and four brothers and she worked on the farm before she was married. So, as you see, I am descended on both sides from farmers, *voilà* !

I was about seven years old when I began at school. We stayed far away from the school, you see – three and a half kilometres away. So I didn't go to school till I was seven. Then at thirteen years of age I started working full-time in Scotland selling onions. So that was only six years I was at school, from seven to thirteen.

But, as I say, the first time I went to Leith to sell onions I was still at school. It was during the school summer holidays. At that time, well, I worked on the farm sometimes helping my father, because, you see, we had not much money. I liked to work. Well, I had a friend who said to me, 'Come with me to sell onions in Britain.' It was 1929. I was just twelve years old.

Scotland was far away from Brittany. Well, we went that first time from Plouescat to Roscoff. It was August. It was always August you went away to sell the onions. We brought the onions from my father's farm with the horses to the boat at Roscoff.

It was a small boat, a sailing boat with no motors and no nothing at all! It took us fifteen days to sail from Roscoff to Leith because the weather was bad. The sails of the boat were torn twice by the winds. But a small British boat came and took us into the port of Leith. We stayed in the port for a day to repair the sails by sewing the torn pieces together. After that we were OK. It was a long voyage, well – two weeks!

But I wasn't seasick on that voyage. I was already accustomed to sailing. Oh, it was fine, fine. It was always my wish to sail. Every year after that I went with the boat with the onions from Roscoff to Leith, because I liked the sea, I liked it so much. I was a good sailor!

Well, that was the first year I went. And then the next year, in 1930, when I was thirteen, I left school. I went again then with my friend to work as an onion seller at Leith. That was my first full-time job. I worked in Scotland as an Onion Johnny for six or seven years after that.

At Leith I lived with other Onion Johnnies in a shop with three floors at No. 18 Quality Street. It was a big shop. There were nine or ten of us Johnnies. There were no beds – only straw to lie on. We slept all together in a row on the straw, like herrings or sardines! I was the youngest and I was in the middle of the row. You had covers, blankets. But we also had a sack or bag to sleep in – a sleeping bag. Oh, it was very comfortable. We were there all together, quite warm on the straw, so we didn't feel cold. Oh, that was OK. I liked that. Then you had a little table to eat on. The kitchen was quite small. There was a tap with running water, and there was a wc downstairs – a flush toilet.

The toilet reminds me that one time in Quality Street when the big door to the street was open a Scotsman appeared. He just came in and he said, 'Oh! Just a minute.' I told him, 'Hurry up, sir.' Then when he came out from our toilet he said, 'It's OK now.'

On the ground floor at No. 18 Quality Street there was – nothing. It was on the first floor that we lived along with the onions and everything. You had trunks to put your linen and some bigger things in.

We were ten Onion Johnnies, at that time, I think. There were two bosses among the ten. The bosses were OK. I was the youngest of the Johnnies, I was very young. But the year after that there was another young one who came on the boat. He was only twelve years old. He was the son of a man called Guyader, who lived at the port of Santec, near Roscoff in Britanny. So that boy was the youngest then.

One of the Johnnies worked in the shop all the time stringing the onions. It was always the same man. He was

Yan Guyader, one of two brothers. He just sat in the shop and strung the onions. He was quick at that. Well, sometimes – not the first year I was there but the second year – I helped him myself. I learned to string the onions, so I was able to help him a little bit. The other Guyader brother he had to go out and sell the onions.

The two bosses they went away in the morning on Monday and stayed away till Saturday. One of them went, I remember, from Edinburgh to Glasgow with onions on the train to sell there. He didn't sell onions in Leith or Edinburgh, but in Glasgow. It was Saturday when he came home to Quality Street again. In fact, the two bosses went to Glasgow and to other places. I don't know where they sold the onions in Glasgow because I didn't know anything much about Glasgow.

But one day one of the bosses, Yvon Yvonique, who was my boss, told me to go with him to Glasgow for a day or two. So I said to him, 'Well, I'll go and see you there but I'm going with my bicycle.' I don't know how many kilometres it was between Leith and Glasgow – maybe 80 or 90, or about 50 miles – but I went to Glasgow with my bicycle. I loaded my onions on to the bicycle. I had onions hanging from the handlebars and others hanging behind the seat – onions at the back and the front!

Well, it was quite a flat road from Edinburgh to Glasgow, oh, well, there weren't many hills. I set off very early in the morning. Well, I sold my onions in Glasgow. I was there two nights. We stayed at a lodging and did our own cooking there. We stayed for the night and next day we sold onions again. That was a Friday, I think, and I came back home again to Leith on the next day with the train. By then I had the money to pay the train fare!

Well, the Onion Johnnies I worked with in Leith were friendly and helpful to me. The older ones looked on me, I think, as a kind of son because at first I was the youngest –

and I was in the middle of the row when at night we went to sleep on the straw!

The Johnnies in that shop at No.18 Quality Street came and went a bit. They changed from time to time. We stayed there, well, about five months at a time. Some went home then and didn't return, and others – like myself as a young boy in 1929–30 – -came who hadn't been there before.

It was about the 13th or 20th of August every year, around the time of the Feast of the Assumption, that you left Brittany and went to Britain – in my case, to Leith. The onions weren't ready before then. You must have seed, you see. So once the onions were ready in August or July you set off from Brittany for Leith. Oh, every year was the same for us. The bosses set off for Britain eight days before the *ouvriers*, the ordinary Onion Johnnies, so they could make arrangements about the shop, about the necessary papers and all that before our arrival.

Well, from August you worked selling the onions then September, October, November, December – five months. We would come home sometimes in time for Christmas, other times we didn't come home until the end of January.

The first year I worked selling the onions at Leith was not too hard. But the second year was very hard. At first I just worked with a baton. That was a long stick on your shoulder, from which the onions hung in strings or bunches. You carried only one baton. That was enough! I don't know, but I think the weight of the onions we carried for selling was about 25 or 30 kilogrammes – about 50 to 60 pounds. But we didn't go very far away with that load! And I used to ask the people, the customers, 'Please, you want some onions?' – because, you know, the weight . . . Of course, the weight was heaviest at the beginning of the day. Then, well, once you sold some it was lighter after that. Of course, when we were tired we used to put the baton on to the other shoulder to carry it. But the first eight days I was selling the onions my shoulder was sore, *oh, là, là!* As sailors say, I had a list to port!

That first year I was there there was a little cart, as well as the baton, a little wooden cart with two wheels. It was big enough for the job, though. With a pal, a *copain*, I went one day with the cart for a dozen kilometres trying to sell the onions in it. But we didn't sell any onions at all. Wherever we went we seemed to find that people already had onions in their houses. Well, when we got back to Quality Street, the boss took me by the ear. I still remember that. I thought it wasn't my fault we hadn't sold any onions. I knew nothing at all at that time. Well, later I said to the boss, 'You'll not have any need to take me by the ear again.' After that I went off working on my own and it was far better. Then I was responsible only for myself and for no one else.

We started work, well, about eight o'clock in the morning, after our breakfast. In those days in Britain there were more people at home. Women weren't working so much away from home in those days. So the wives – every one was at home. It was the wife who opened the door and bought the onions. When she opened the door, I would say, 'Good morning.' The wife would look at the onions and would say, 'Well, I don't want any this morning.' So then I would say, 'Thank you very much. I'll see you next time.' 'Yes,' the wife would say. So that's how I got a lot of customers after that as time went on. When I went to their door they would buy onions from me every time. I was very polite, *voilà*! I was very diplomatic! It was good because the Scots and the Scots women were very, very good. It was good for me, too, because I was very young. I think they were sympathetic to me.

When we sold the onions then we came back to the shop at Quality Street and took some more. That was in the days when I was working just with a baton over the shoulder. Sometimes we sold the onions quickly. But sometimes it was one or two o'clock in the afternoon before we went back to the shop. By that time I was very tired and ready for something to eat and drink. When we went back to the shop for more onions we would eat something while the Johnny in the shop strung some more onions for us. It was three years after I began working as an Onion Johnny that I got a bicycle. A bicycle was much better, much easier than going with the baton, and you could take more onions to sell, too.

We had regular customers who bought the onions. Some days it was easier to sell the onions than other days. There were days when we would go into one place, maybe Mondays, and on, say, Thursdays we would go to another one. We did that kind of round sometimes every eight days. Then we would go back again.

I remember some of the places in Leith and Edinburgh where I sold onions. I didn't stay in Leith all the time selling them. Granton – that was the first, it wasn't far from Leith. So I would start at Granton and then go to Abbeyhill and then other places after that. I think it was in Gorgie where I found it more difficult to sell onions than most other places. I don't know but I think maybe people in Gorgie were different. They were working people, *ouvriers*, there and very poor some of them. So it was more difficult to sell onions in Gorgie than in, say, Morningside. Morningside was very, very good. There was more money there. But I didn't stop going to Gorgie with onions because it was more difficult there.

As I say, it was three years before I got a bicycle. It had turned down handlebars. But I put a baton under the handlebars and put strings of onions on it. And I made a net also for the wheels to stop the onions from touching the spokes. It was an old bike, a Scottish bike. You could carry more onions on the bike with its two wheels than you could manage with a baton. The bike was fine. You walked a little with it at first and then after you'd sold some onions it was easier. Once I got the bike, one of my customers who'd seen me before always with that baton asked me, 'Hello, what about your shoulder?' 'Oh, well,' I said, 'it's OK now.'

Jean Milin

The bicycles made the selling of the onions so much easier, and once we got the bikes we got farther. We were sometimes 20 kilometres from home in Quality Street, oh, easy. I went to Musselburgh, for instance. And, as I say, I went to Gorgie, Morningside – that was my usual place – Bruntsfield, Fairmilehead, I went there, too. To go to away up from Leith to Fairmilehead was very hard. But to come home from Fairmilehead – well, shoooo! Almost straight downhill to Leith!

Sometimes we took the tramway. We put the onions, with the baton or the bike, inside the tram beside the driver. But he didn't take any money at all from us. We didn't pay any fares. It was always free. That was very, very good. And then sometimes when I went to Morningside or somewhere like that, which was a long way from Leith, I took a train. I put my bicycle with the onions on the train. The train was very, very good for getting to Morningside, because the station there was just beside the main street. There were a lot of customers there.

When you went to Edinburgh, to Princes Street, the main street, well, it was about two and a half kilometres maybe from Leith. It was a long way up – up Leith Walk, and then up Leith Street, which was quite a hill. When you got up there you were very tired. So we used to stop there sometimes for ten minutes to rest. I remember one day I was resting there and there was some kind of fête on in Princes Street. The Queen Mother was there. She saw me. She put her hand to her head. I would have liked to have spoken to her, I would! But we went off in different directions.

And then one year in the 1930s my younger brother René came to Scotland and worked for a year with me at Leith. René had a bike, too, with the onions. He made up the bike himself when he came to Leith. But his bike didn't have any brakes! One day he and I came to a roundabout where there was a policeman standing. I was able to use my brakes but

René of course had none to use. Well, he went right round the policeman on his bike with the onions. Well, I called out, 'I'm sorry, I'm sorry.' The policeman said, 'Oh, all right, all right.' Later on René went off to Algeria to do his military service in the French army and he died there.

All the words in English I could speak when I first went to sell onions in Scotland were 'Penny, sweeties, please.' That was what my friend from school whom I went first to Leith with told me to ask for. Just those three words. So the first day I was going to sell the onions, well, I couldn't speak English at all. I think we sold the onions for 6d. or something like that. So a woman customer asked me, 'How much? How much?' And she counted out one, two, three, four, five, six, and gave me the money. But a month after that my English was coming along! I learned quickly.

Sometimes people would give you money for the onions and tell you to keep the change for yourself. It didn't happen often, but some people said that. Sometimes they would give you a penny from the change from the price.

Sometimes, too, customers gave us things to eat or drink: tea, milk, bread and jam, tea and biscuits, an apple, sweeties – sweeties especially when I was a very young boy. Sometimes you got a cup of tea or milk. Sometimes you got eggs and everything – 'Take that.'

And then in Morningside there was a woman customer and her husband. They invited me every Sunday to go and eat a meal with them. The husband was an electrician. He gave me the money for the train. I took a friend with me, too. I can't remember now the name of that couple at Morningside, it's such a long time ago. And in Granton I had two other people like that. Granton wasn't far from home in Quality Street, so I went there sometimes on a Saturday night to eat a meal with that couple, too. It wasn't very often that Onion Johnnies received invitations like that. They were good people, too, that Granton couple. They were poor people. But I left them onions during the week and on Saturday they paid me the money. Sometimes they gave me fish to bring home to eat at Quality Street. The husband was a fisherman at Granton.

I had Scottish friends at Portobello, too, a husband and wife. Sometimes when I was very late working I stayed there to eat with them at Portobello. Then there was a woman customer and her husband at Abbeyhill and I was sometimes invited there to eat on a Sunday evening. They had plenty of money. The husband was a commander in the British navy. He died just two years ago.

So I had customers who were friends at Morningside, Granton, Abbeyhill and Portobello. I liked the Scottish people, I still like them. One day at Plouescat not long ago I heard a man asking about something. But the French boy he asked didn't understand. So I said to the man, 'You're Scottish?' 'Yes,' he said. 'Where do you come from?', I asked. 'Portobello.' 'Oh, Jésu Christ.' So it turned out that he has a house near Plouescat, at Pors-Guen.

As I say, we began work every day about 8 o'clock, after breakfast. Sometimes a customer would take one or two bunches, sometimes more, for her children. And then we would come back early to the shop in Quality Street. So we would string some onions in the shop and then we went out and sold them. We kept taking the onions away and selling them. Oh, at that time, in the 1930s, we had no hours! We just came back to the shop and took out more onions and sold them. That was the life every day.

We didn't have any sort of trade union of Onion Johnnies.

Usually, though, we would finish selling onions about 7 o'clock in the evening. But we would work at home in Quality Street when we came in then, stringing the onions. We would do that for some time before we went to bed. We were preparing strings and bunches of onions for the day after, you see, so we'd be ready in the morning for going out to sell them.

In the evening, when we came back to the shop in Quality Street, and before we worked stringing the onions, we had our supper. The butcher came every Saturday with meat for us. We ate steak. He was a good butcher, it was good meat. And we ate a lot of onions, too, with the steak!

We went to bed very early, about nine o'clock, because we were tired, you know. We were walking a lot, you see, with the onions. So when you came back in the evening, had your supper, strung some onions, then you went to bed!

I didn't go out in the evening during the week. And you worked on a Saturday, so I never went to a football match. I remember once – it was in 1933, I think – a Frenchman came to sing in Edinburgh: Maurice Chevalier. I went to the theatre in Edinburgh then and saw him there. He was a good singer. I spoke to Maurice Chevalier then.[6] I spoke to him in English because he spoke English, too, you know. He spoke very good English. He performed in films where he spoke English. Then I went to see another man, an Englishman, at the theatre and he was a very nice singer, too. These were the only times I went to the theatre in Edinburgh. But I never went to the cinema. We just stayed at home in the shop at Quality Street and helped the man to string the onions.

Sometimes the Johnnies went to the pub on a Friday night, but more usually it was a Saturday night they went. But there wasn't much drinking. I didn't go of course when I was so young. The young ones like me could go and get coffee. Sometimes the men brought something back home to Quality Street with them from the pub to drink on Sunday.

On Sunday we went to church – every Sunday. It was not a Catholic but a Protestant church in Leith we went to. I was Catholic, and so were the other Johnnies at Quality Street. But we went every Sunday to the Protestant church in Leith, not far from our home in Quality Street. The pastor, the minister, gave us whisky! It was not a lot but, you know, some. There were two Catholic churches but they were further away. But we stayed every year with the Protestant church because the minister came sometimes to buy onions from us. So, you know, he asked me, 'Will you come to the church?' He was very nice, very, very nice. Well, we sold him onions. It's possible the Catholic priest knew that we went to the Protestant church but, well, everyone is free!

Well, after we went every Sunday morning to the Protestant church we went to swim. We swam just about the docks in Leith. The water there was very clean at that time. Sometimes we went to Portobello to swim, too. All the Onion Johnnies sometimes went there, we all liked to swim. It was very nice there. It was really only on a Sunday that we had some leisure time. But even on a Sunday, you know, after we'd been at church we worked for an hour and a half in the afternoon helping the man who strung the onions a little. We had a kind of race, a sort of competition then to see who could string the most. I usually beat the others at that because I was so accustomed to it as every day I did a little of that work to help the onion-stringer.

We strung the onions with straw or with hay. There was a special way of stringing them. The biggest onion in a string was called the captain, *le capitaine*. That was the big one, the captain. So the captain was at the top. Then after that you have the smaller onions, the sailors – *les marins*. So the smallest were at the bottom of the string, and the *le grand* – the captain – at the top. Sometimes people asked us about the big onion. So we told them, 'That's the captain.' Customers would look at or touch the big one, the captain. It was nicer than the other smaller ones, the sailors, *les marins*. The captain looked nice and big. That was the tradition.

The onions we sold arrived at Leith, oh, twice in a season. When I first went there in 1929–30 the onions were taken off the boat by Scotsmen with a horse. There were two horses –

but no cart – used to bring the onions to the shop in Quality Street. It was a good place to keep the onions because there were plenty of windows there. The onions were well aired and had plenty of light. It was good for the onions to have light, it wouldn't have been good for them to have been kept in the dark. Sometimes we turned them over, moved them about a bit in the store, so they didn't go soft. If they went soft you couldn't sell them.

Well, we Onion Johnnies were always working. It was a hard life. And we didn't receive much money at that time when we were very young. I'm going to tell you something about the payment. The first year I went to Leith we had no money while we were in Scotland – just when we came back home at the end of the season. So my mother and father came the 20 or so kilometres from Plouescat, where we lived, to Roscoff to take my money, because I was very young. The year after that I got more money than the first year because, well, the boss, you know, if you were working OK for him, well, he gave you a bit more money. So that second time when my mother saw the money I had she was pleased, because she didn't have much money at home at Plouescat. My money from selling the onions at Leith was a big help to my mother and father. So all the money I received as payment as an Onion Johnny I gave to my parents when I came home to Plouescat at the end of the season. I can't remember now how much money I was paid. The franc was different then from what it is now. I don't remember too much about it, it's such a long time ago.[7] But my father and mother were very pleased to see the money I had received. They felt it was quite a lot of money that I had earned. I gave it all to them.

Well, I worked as an Onion Johnny at Leith for six or seven years, from 1929–30. At the end of 1936, when I was 19½, I went into the navy just two or three months ahead of my call-up for military service. At that time you had to do three years if you went into the navy in France. I had been to sea several times with my father and I was on the register of sailors. I was accustomed to the sea, to the English Channel, to the dangers of the sea and all that. My idea was that once my navy service was finished I would go into the merchant navy. But, of course, by the time my naval service was up the 1939–45 War began. I was out for just about a month when the war broke out. So then I had to stay in the navy. I served 22 years altogether. In the navy I became an English interpreter. Brest was my home base.

During the early part of the war I was in the Narvik campaign in Norway in the spring of 1940. At Narvik we had the task of taking off the staff of the French embassy during the night. All that night we were bombed by the Germans until we reached Dunkirk. But we weren't hit.[8]

I was at the evacuation from Dunkirk, too, in the summer of 1940. There some of the German troops were disguised as nuns. Oh, Dunkirk was a disaster – a disaster and a miracle. One never understood how so many of our troops were able to get away from there. I saw British soldiers dying in the evening on the sands and on the dykes. One saw them dying there – French, British, everyone.[9]

After Dunkirk and the fall of France in June 1940 I remained at home at Plouescat in Britanny. I still had connections with the navy. I refused to support Marshal Pétain. Anyway I was able to hide at my wife's place.[10]

My wife and I were married in 1940. Then I joined the Resistance. We saw arms from Britain landed by parachute – eight tons of them in the first drop, and a further eight tons later. And there was a British, a French, and an American officer whom I had to receive. We went into action on D-Day, the 6th of June 1944, when the Allied landings took place in Normandy. Afterwards I remained for a time with the Americans at Brest. After the war I didn't go back to being an Onion Johnny in Scotland! I remained in the French navy until I retired from it in 1960.

Onion Johnnies

Well, looking back all those years ago to the 1930s, when as a boy I worked as an Onion Johnny at Leith, I have no regrets at all. And I learned English! But I tell you frankly that I still feel very attached to the Onion Johnnies whom I know. I esteem them all very much. In fact, every year I go to a reunion of Johnnies out of the respect I have for them. It's held in the month of August. That was the very month I first left Roscoff in 1929 to sail to Leith to sell onions. I would very much like to go back now to Leith, to see the place again.

ANNA GOURLET

I first went to Scotland – to Leith – to work with the onions
when I was about 11½ years old. That was in 1930 or 1931.
But I really began to sell the onions as an Onion Johnny – or
Onion Jenny – when I was about 13 years old.

I was born in 1919 at Roscoff, on the coast of Brittany. My
father was an Onion Johnny. He was born in Roscoff, too. I
don't know when first he became a Johnny, whether it was
when he was still just a young boy or whether he began only
after the 1914–18 War, about the time I was born. But he
worked also as an *emballeur*, a packer, in a vegetable store at
St Pol de Léon, five kilometres down the coast from Roscoff. I
don't know how many years he worked there on the vegetables. But he worked there in the winters, before he went to
Scotland to sell onions, and again after he came home at the
end of the onion-selling season.

When he went to Scotland as an Onion Johnny my father
left Roscoff on the onion boat. I never went on the onion
boat, I always went by train from Roscoff. My father was
always an Onion Johnny at Leith and Edinburgh but he also
sold the onions in the country beyond Edinburgh. I don't
remember where he went in the countryside in Scotland, but I
do know he went to Glasgow sometimes to sell onions. But he
was always away from our shop, our home, in Leith during
the week selling onions and he only came back home on
Saturdays. So he was never at home there except at the
weekends.

My mother also lived at our shop in Leith and worked on

the onions there. She strung the onions into bunches but she didn't sell them. She selected the onions for stringing and strung them. As my father was away working elsewhere all week she was accustomed to being alone during the week. My mother worked hard. She was a kind person.

And then my young brother François, who was six years younger than me, was in Scotland at Leith, too, later on working as an Onion Johnny. When he first went to Leith he was only a little boy, and in fact he went to school in Leith from 1932 to 1934. So all of us in our family, my father, mother, me and my young brother, were all in Leith at that time.

I myself began school in Roscoff at the age of five in 1924. I left school when I was about 11½ years old and it was then, as soon as I left school, I went with my parents to Scotland to work at the onions. That was in 1930–1. It was my first job after I left the school.

Well, as I say, my father went to Leith on the onion boat from Roscoff, but my mother and I went on the train. I was very excited. We went from Roscoff to Paris on the train, then from Paris to Dieppe. We took the ferry across the Channel from Dieppe to Newhaven. That took about four hours, I think. And then the train again from Newhaven to London, and from London to Edinburgh. Oh, it was a long journey, but I wasn't tired out. I was young! It was quite an adventure for me as a girl of 11½ years old. But I liked that. And I wasn't seasick at all. The sea was quite calm. I can't remember now if there were other Onion Johnnies who travelled with us on the train or on the ferry from Dieppe. It's a long time ago, and you forget some things.

At Leith my mother and father had a shop which was also our home in Quality Street. Later on we were at No. 8 Bernard Street. But at Quality Street it was a very simple place. There was really nothing there to begin with. But we managed to store the onions there and to sleep there, too.

There weren't any separate rooms in the place in Quality Street: it was a shop, a store place. You made rooms by building up the sacks of onions as walls. It wasn't exactly the Ritz Hotel! But you made a room with the sacks. Later the onions were on the floor. And then that was it, that's all there was, *voilà*!

There was no toilet, nothing, in the shop in Quality Street. The 'toilet' was in the 'room' made with the sacks of onions. I don't remember clearly what water supply there was but there must have been a tap. We slept on the floor to begin with and then later on there were iron bedsteads.

I was only 11½, as I say, when I first went to Leith with my parents but I never went to school there. My young brother François did go to school there a bit later on, in 1932. François, being younger than me, was more spoiled! That's true! He was a little spoiled boy for sure!

Well, working with the onions was quite a hard life. But I liked it, I really did like it. And then in Leith at that time there were other Onion Johnnies from Brittany who were about the same age as my father and mother and some of them had their children with them, too. So there were other French Breton children there that I knew and so I had pals. One I remember was Yvon Tanguy.

At first, for the first year or more I was at Leith, I worked in the shop, helping my mother and father by selecting and stringing the onions. I selected them and my mother strung them. I did the straw, too. While my mother and I were in the shop doing that my father was away out in the countryside selling the onions.

Then when I was about thirteen – that would be in 1932 – I began to go out and sell the onions. My mother and father were kind people. They certainly didn't force me to go out and sell the onions. I liked doing that.

I didn't have a bike to begin with. So I went out carrying strings or bunches of the onions in my hands. The baton was the old way the Johnnies used to carry the onions. But I never had a baton to carry the onions, just my hands. The onions were heavy – but I was young! And sometimes I went on the tramcar with the onions, so that made things easier. When I sold the onions I had I went back to the shop and got more. I liked doing that work, in fact, I adored doing that.

But I soon got a bike to take the onions on. It was a woman's bike, just a normal-sized bike, a French bike. It was better with the bike than carrying the onions in my hands, it was much easier with the two wheels to carry them. I never had any punctures or problems like that with the bike. It's true I fell off my bike several times when I was working as an Onion Johnny. But I never had any real accidents with the bike. Sometimes if the bike wheels went into the tram lines you would fall off. And I remember one time when I was selling onions on my bike at Portobello. My young brother François was with me and I ended up against a wall and he was on the ground. But we weren't hurt, I was skinned a bit but nothing worse than that.

The onions were heavy, of course, when I set off on the bike. At first I walked a little bit with them then I got on the bike. I was soon accustomed to doing that. It became a habit. I don't know how many onions I carried on my bike when I set off from the shop in Quality Street or Bernard Street in the morning. But there were certainly quite a lot of bunches! There were bunches on the handlebars and on the carrier at the back of the bike. Oh, there were well over a hundred onions altogether! What a weight they were! That's why I walked a bit, as I say, with the bike to begin with. But as a young girl I was quite strong.

I sold the onions around Edinburgh. But I didn't go too far away from our shop in Quality Street or Bernard Street in Leith. I sold them in Trinity, Portobello, Granton, Leith, Abbeyhill, Easter Road, at Leith Links, and some other places in Edinburgh. I sold them in Princes Street, but I don't remember now the names of the other streets where I sold them. But I sold them in Musselburgh, too. Musselburgh was about eight kilometres from Leith.

When I began selling the onions my father didn't give me a list of customers where I could sell them. I decided myself where I was going to go to sell the onions. Well, I visited all the districts and then after that I had lists of customers. I didn't sell the onions to butchers' shops or to hotels but just to ordinary people.

What I did was I went into the tenement stairs. The stairs had four or five landings in them. There were bells for the houses at the street door at the bottom of the stair. So at the bottom of the stair I rang the bell of someone in the stair who wasn't one of my customers! I would hear somebody grumbling up above. But then the stair door opened and in I went to the stair. I could kid them on. Well, I went up the stair, five, six flats. I rang the bell and *voilà* somebody was in and opened their door to me. I wouldn't do now what I did then as a young girl! But I never rang the stair bell of a customer – it was always somebody else's bell I rang. And she would grumble about it! But I would then go up the landings. I knew exactly who my customers were in the stair, but of course I tried to sell the onions to people there who had not been customers before. That's how I built up my list of customers!

When I rang the bell at a door on the landings I didn't step forward. I just stood on the landing. I never went into anyone's house. I had been warned about that by my mother and father and I never did go into a customer's house. But I was never attacked, never.

People, the Scottish people, were polite and were very kind. But I never went into anyone's house. I was never invited, either by myself or to go with my parents, into anyone's house in Leith or Edinburgh. That never happened. No one asked me to come in for tea. I never made any friends among young Scots girls. I wanted to but I was advised to be careful about that.

Onion Johnnies

You had to sell all the onions you had before you went home in the evening. But I wasn't obliged to take any particular number or weight of onions with me to sell. I just took what I wanted to. I never had any difficulty in selling what I took out with me before I went home. I think it was easier for a young girl like me to sell the onions than it was for the men Onion Johnnies. In Scotland no one was afraid of a young girl selling onions! It was a question of charm, *voilà*!

I didn't wear any special clothing for selling the onions. I wore a short jacket and a jumper, a skirt and stockings. Round my neck I wore a cravat, and I always had my beret on, as I was in the habit of wearing one. I wore shoes. And I always had my raincoat on my bike on the carrier. I didn't have a bag to put the money I took for selling the onions, I kept it in my pockets. My skirt had pockets in it. I never carried a lot of money on me because I went back home every day between about midday and two o'clock for something to eat, and left the money there that I had taken in the morning.

In the early years I was in Leith I remember there were some other Breton Onion Johnnies at Quality Street. I remember going into stairs and seeing other Johnnies on the landings selling their onions. But I was the only girl who sold the onions.

As an Onion Johnny or Onion Jenny I didn't have any regular hours of work. You just had to sell the onions you had before you went home. So I was finished and went home when I had sold all the onions I had with me.

At first at Leith, when I was working with my mother in the shop selecting and stringing the onions, I used to start work about eight o'clock in the morning and work until late in the evening, perhaps about seven o'clock. Then when I started to sell the onions I began work after I got up in the morning. In the shop and when I was selling I worked six days a week, Monday to Saturday – but not on Sundays. I finished work a bit earlier on Saturdays, perhaps about five o'clock.

On Sundays, you did just a little bit of work. On Sunday afternoons I helped to select and string some of the onions if there was work of that sort to be done.

During the day when I was out selling the onions I went home for something to eat, oh, between about midday and two o'clock. Sometimes I didn't get home during the week until 10 o'clock at night. On those occasions I was a bit nervous. But, as I say, I was never attacked and never robbed, never. I never had any of my onions stolen either. So I wasn't afraid, unless I was working late at night. I think people rather felt sorry for me! Everybody knew me, I was well known as an Onion Johnny or Onion Jenny in Leith. Sometimes young fellows on the pavement whistled at me. Sometimes people would call out to me, 'Onion Johnny!' or 'Ingan Johnny!' That's all they ever said. When they called 'Ingan Johnny', I just said to them: 'Shurrruppp!' I paid no attention to them but just passed on. *Voilà*!

I never had any wages as an Onion Johnny – nothing. I handed over to my parents all the money I took for selling the onions. But what I did was I sold the onions I had for just a little more! I kept a little of the money then so that I could go to the cinema. I never asked my mother's permission to do that! And of course my father was away from the shop all week working in the countryside. *Quand le chat n'est pas là la souris danse*! When the cat's away the mouse will play! So I did what I pleased!

I didn't smoke and I didn't eat sweets. But I loved the cinema. I went to the cinema almost every day. Sometimes I went to the cinema two or three times a day! I sold all my onions before I went and went home with my bike first. Once I had sold all the onions I had I was free to go. On Saturdays, as I say, I finished work earlier and went to the cinema. I went to the Alhambra cinema in Leith. It was on the road from Leith to Edinburgh – Leith Walk. There was another cinema, too, I used to go to but I can't remember its name now. It was only a penny or two pennies to get into the cinema in those days. I always went on my own. But my mother always knew where I was, she always knew I was at the cinema.[11]

On Sundays I went to mass in the morning. My parents were religious and went regularly to mass, and so did I. I never found any difficulty about being a Catholic in Leith. I have been told about John Cormack and the Protestant Action movement who were active in Leith in the 1930s at the time my parents and I were there, but I don't remember that man or his movement.[12] On Sunday afternoons, as I've said, we worked in the shop for a time when it was necessary, selecting and stringing the onions.

Well, I worked at Leith as an Onion Johnny or Jenny for about eight years. Then when I was twenty I got married. That was in June 1939. My husband came from Rieç-sur-Bélon in Brittany. That's about 130 kilometres from Roscoff and near the coast of southern Brittany. He was a sailor in the French navy. We met at Rieç-sur-Bélon at the wedding of my cousin, Anna Perron, who married a friend of my husband's. My husband asked me to dance. Afterwards we wrote to each other for about a year. So we were married in June 1939, just before the war broke out. I stopped then working as an Onion Johnny at Leith and went back to France. From then on I followed my husband.

We weren't separated even during the war. We were always together. We spent five years on Corsica at Ajaccio during the war. My husband was still in the French navy throughout the war. They were all sort of sailors in disguise. They were without ships. My husband wore civilian clothes.[13] We lived in the countryside. Food was very, very scarce. You had to live as best you could. You went looking for chestnuts to eat. You killed animals for food. The wife of the commandant gave us a cat. We had to eat that, too. What a life! But we survived, although my husband was arrested at one stage by the Italians, who were in occupation then of Ajaccio until the surrender of Italy in 1943, when the Germans took control in Corsica. However, my husband managed to get away. So we remained at Ajaccio till the end of the war, living in a place five storeys up that we had to climb up to every day as there was no lift! Then after the war was over we came back to Roscoff.[14]

I never went back to work as an Onion Johnny at Leith. In fact, I didn't have a job at all after I was married. I always followed my husband, and of course I worked in our house.

Looking back now to the 1930s when I was an Onion Johnny at Leith, I have no regrets. I wasn't afraid to start the job – and no one ever attacked me. I loved Scotland and I was really pleased to be working at selling the onions. And I went to the cinema every day, whenever I wanted to. My mother was busy stringing the onions but she always knew I had gone to the cinema.

FRANÇOIS PERRON

Because I went to Scotland with my father and mother I started school in Leith at St Mary's School in Henderson Street in 1932, when I was seven. I had learned to speak English even before I went to school there. So I didn't have any difficulty at St Mary's School in speaking English. That was a result of my father working in Leith. He was an Onion Johnny there.[15]

I was born in Roscoff in Brittany on 18 November 1925. My father was at first a farm labourer. He worked on the farms around Roscoff, but he became an Onion Johnny at Leith, and then he also worked the other months of the year in a vegetable factory at St Pol de Léon, near Roscoff. He was born about 1886. I don't know when he first became an Onion Johnny. It may have been either before the 1914–18 War or soon after it. But he worked in Scotland as a Johnny most of his life, selling the onions. At first he worked in a company of Onion Johnnies at Leith. Then he began working on his own there. He worked always, I think, in or about Edinburgh, and Leith, and maybe in Glasgow, though I don't know for sure if he worked anywhere else. My mother worked with him at Leith, too, for the years I can remember. Then my sister Anna, who is six years older than me, she began working with the onions with my mother and father at Leith when she was about 11 or 12 years old. She worked as an Onion Johnny, too, until she got married in 1939, just before the Second World War began.

My mother before she was married was a *cultivatrice*, a farm worker. Her parents had a little farm at Roscoff, where

66

she belonged. As I've said, when I was a boy my mother worked with my father in Leith at the onions, stringing them for him and for my sister.

My sister had left school at St Pol de Léon before she went to work with my parents in Leith when she was about 11 or 12. She was never at school in Leith. But, as I say, I began at St Mary's School there in 1932 and I was there for two onion-selling seasons, 1932–4. I liked the school. It wasn't common for Onion Johnnies' children to be at school in Leith. But, as I've said, I didn't have any difficulty in speaking English and understanding the teachers and the lessons at St Mary's School. I was obliged to speak English at home. In fact, all the time at home in Leith at that time we spoke only in English or in Breton.

Then after two years at St Mary's I began school at St Pol de Léon in 1934 *en pension* - as a boarder. My family, of course, were still living at Leith during every onion-selling season. Well, I was five years at St Pol de Léon school as a boarder. I liked the school there, too. When I began there I spoke very good English after two years at St Mary's. So when I began and the headteacher spoke to me in French I answered in English, nothing but English!

I left school at St Pol in 1939 when I was 14. I wouldn't have wanted to remain on at school. I wanted to leave so that I could help my parents. It was the custom after leaving school that everyone went to Britain to work with the onions. Anyway I had no ambitions to become a seaman or a fisherman or a railway engine driver or anything like that. You would have needed training for jobs like that. So I was glad to leave school and start to work.

That summer I went to Scotland with my mother and father to work with the onions. We lived and worked in Leith at No. 8 Bernard Street. But I was there only a month – August, 1939 – -when the war broke out. My mother and father and I all came back home to Roscoff. All the Onion Johnnies went back to Brittany.

Onion Johnnies

My father wasn't a reservist in the French army or navy. It was just that the British government said all foreigners had to leave the country. And the French government had an interest in getting people like us back in France again. But my father wasn't called up in the war. He'd be too old by then for that. We spent the war in Roscoff. During the German occupation my father carried on working on the farm. The Germans didn't interfere with him or send him to Germany or anything like that. I worked sometimes two or three days a week, sometimes all week, unloading lorries. I wasn't sent to Germany as a forced labourer by the STO – *Service du Travail Obligatoire* - though those people were around in Brittany.[16]

After the war, in 1949, my father went back to Leith again to work with the onions, and I went with him. My mother came there, too, a year later, in 1950. There were just the three of us. My father was the boss, the *patron*! The three of us worked as a family. My father didn't employ anyone else. It was then that I became an Onion Johnny. I was 24 years old by then.

We lived and worked, as my parents had before the war, at No. 8 Bernard Street. The place was rented to us by a lawyer in Constitution Street, Mr Mossman.[17] No. 8 Bernard Street, which was just along the street from a branch of the Royal Bank of Scotland and the Clydesdale Bank, was a shop but also a house where we lived. The onions were stored down below and the three of us lived upstairs. We were accustomed to that kind of arrangement! Some other Onion Johnnies in Leith lived and slept among the onions, but we didn't.

So from 1949 onwards we went to Leith every August for the onion-selling season. We worked in Leith until we came home to Roscoff again about, oh, sometimes Christmas time, sometimes January or February. We were usually in Leith about five or six months. We didn't come home every year for Christmas, just sometimes. Since we were in Leith working and living as a family I didn't suffer there from homesickness. It was just like being at home as a family in Roscoff.

My father didn't grow the onions himself in Brittany. He bought them from vegetable merchants there. The onions were then brought over on a boat from Roscoff to Leith. The boat was a Dutch boat but I don't remember its name now. It was always the Dutch that brought the onions to us in Leith. Then a lorry – I think it was Young, Glover – brought the onions from Leith docks the same day to our place at No. 8 Bernard Street.[18] There were two loads of onions brought to us each season, one at the beginning and the second one, I think, in November.

As an Onion Johnny at Leith from 1949 I worked six days a week. On a Saturday afternoon you finished early sometimes. And sometimes you worked on a Sunday, though not for long. On weekdays I got up usually about six o'clock in the morning and got washed and ate some breakfast, then set out with the onions to be sold. You started selling them at about, oh, half-past eight or nine o'clock. That was because it took you some time on a bike to get to where you were going from Leith. Every morning I used to go away up Leith Walk, then up Leith Street to Princes Street, and then from there perhaps to Morningside, the Braids, Fairmilehead, Liberton. It was all up hill! Edinburgh is a nice city but it's really very hilly. It was hard going.

So you worked selling the onions until you were finished. Sometimes that was before 12 noon. Other times when I had a lot of onions to sell I finished in the afternoon. You didn't have regular hours, a regular finishing time. Finishing time varied. If it was heavy rain, and you had to wear your oilskins and cap, you would finish a bit earlier. Or if you had to go a longer distance – maybe away up to Fairmilehead, or to Portobello, Joppa, Musselburgh, Cockenzie, Wallyford or Whitecraig – then you might finish earlier, because it would take you an hour or so to get back home to Bernard Street, or you might be later. Then if you were selling the onions nearer home, well, at Newhaven or Blackhall or Leith itself, you would maybe work on till four or five in the afternoon because it's no' very far to go home from there. And then we were working at home late at night, too, stringing the onions.

We strung the onions with straw or rushes. Those made very solid and strong string for the onions. We got straw and rushes from the fields around Edinburgh – near Liberton, for instance. We cut and gathered the rushes ourselves with a sickle. We had the permission of the farmer to do that. We didn't go out into the fields without asking permission.

I never used a baton for selling the onions from. That was the old way. I think my father had used a baton before the war.

I always had a bicycle for the work. I was lucky, I never had any real accidents with my bike. I fell off it occasionally and once I skidded with it on ice, but those things were all very minor. I don't remember any other Onion Johnnies being hurt in any accidents with their bikes.

On the bike the handlebars were loaded with onions hanging from them, and there were onions loaded over the back wheel, too. Oh, the bike was heavy with the onions when you set out first in the morning. I'm not sure of the weight, but I think it would be more than 30 kilos – maybe 50 kilos: about a hundredweight.

And then of course there was garlic, too, that you took on the bike to sell, as well as the onions. And you had *piclels* – that's a Breton word. It meant small onions. You would eat the *piclels* with bread. I didn't take carrots or cabbages or shallots with me on the bike to sell, just onions, garlic and *piclels*. The people who bought garlic were shops – butchers – and some houses where there were French people living. There were a lot of French people living in Edinburgh and Leith then. And then there was the French Consulate and the French Institute in Randolph Crescent. There weren't many Scotch folk bought garlic.

I remember some of the places I sold the onions in and around Edinburgh were, as I say, Morningside, the Braids, Fairmilehead, Marchmont, around the Meadows, Newington, Liberton, Blackhall, Newhaven, Leith, Portobello, Joppa, Musselburgh, Prestonpans, Cockenzie, North Berwick, Wallyford, Whitecraig, Dalkeith. At Portobello you had the sea, and after Musselburgh you had the sea all the way along to North Berwick.

We had about 500 customers. You went round them about once every month. But some people it was two weeks because they wanted more onions in two weeks. Other ones you went every three weeks, and others again every four weeks. They didn't all buy our onions every time! Sometimes they told you, 'No, no' today. Next time when you come.' But we had good customers. When I went to their door I was sure to sell onions there. Yes, we had good customers. They bought onions every time and some bought two or three lots.

I remember some good customers I had. Mrs E. Logan was one. Her husband was a painter. They lived in the house after Mount Vernon Catholic cemetery at Liberton. They had a sort of Judas door, a door with a spyhole in it. The boss of Mount Vernon cemetery I remember was a Scotchman. His name was Shepherd, and his wife was a French lady. They were the caretakers, the *concièrges*, at the cemetery. It was easier to speak to the lady, Mrs Shepherd, in French, of course. Mr Shepherd was a good man. There was a lot of people in Scotland spoke French. And there were some young people at school who liked to speak French to me when I came to the houses with the onions. I was never asked to go to a school and speak to the children there about my work as an Onion Johnny.

One of our customers was Gumley, who lived in a big, big house.[19] And then students were in Edinburgh all year and they were good customers, too. A lot of them lived in apartments in flats in Marchmont, at the Meadows, and Newington. There was a dentist at Musselburgh who was a good customer. The dentist's was a big house and there were a lot of people working there. The lady there bought a great many onions. Then we had good customers on Fridays or Saturdays at Wallyford and Whitecraig – the miners. That's when they got their pay, on a Friday! And some got their pay on a Thursday. But if you went there on a Monday – *ce n'était pas la peine*! It wasn't worthwhile!

Some of the small hotels bought our onions, and some restaurants, and there was a butcher on the corner of a street at Newington who was a good customer. He used our onions for *charcuterie* – cooked meats, and for tripe and mince, as flavouring.

Sometimes I was invited into customers' houses. Sometimes that happened. You were invited to drink a cup of tea. I had friends among my Scots customers. And there was a French family, too, with whom I was friendly.

I never found any hostility in Scotland. People were correct and very polite. Oh, sometimes kids would call out to me, 'The Onion Man!' 'Ingan Johnny!' But that was all. There was never anything more serious than that, never. Onion Johnnies never had any difficulty in Scotland or England either. You were well regarded there.

It's a long time ago now but I think the price of our onions was about five or six shillings for a bunch, and 2s.9d. for a half bunch – *une ficelle*, a string. There would be half a dozen onions in a string. Onions were cheaper than that if you bought them in a shop. Our Breton onions were dearer – but they were better! Dearer but better. Our onions were better because they were *plus doux* – sweeter. And they were less hard, more tender, as well as having a better taste. Their smell was better, too.

As an Onion Johnny I didn't wear any special clothes. I just wore trousers and a corduroy jacket, shoes. I never wore wooden clogs for cycling. My father used to wear a beret but I didn't. As I say, when it rained I had my oilskins and cap.

After the war, when my father and mother and I went back

to sell the onions at Leith, there were about 25 or 30 Onion Johnnies there. There were other Johnnies at Glasgow, Dunfermline, Dundee, Aberdeen, Buckie, Inverness.

There wasn't a trade union of Johnnies, certainly not at Leith. I was never in a union, not even at St Pol de Léon. There was an association of Johnnies at Roscoff and its purpose was to provide help. The association had a card and if somebody stopped you in Scotland you could show the card, a kind of licence to sell the onions. I think it was the parliament in London which gave the Onion Johnnies the licence to sell their onions in Britain. The Johnnies' job was special. It was authorised in that way.

Something else I never had was holidays. We never went away for a holiday, either in Scotland or at home in Roscoff.

As I say, we didn't work so much on Sundays. I went to St Mary's, the Catholic church in Leith, but not every Sunday. On Sunday I often went for a walk, usually round the port of Leith, the old harbour. There were a lot of ships there then. Sometimes, too, I went to Portobello or Musselburgh and to the Pentland Hills. I liked walking when I had time. So on Sunday you went out sometimes, but not during the week. Then I liked to go cycling, too, round the countryside a bit. I wasn't a reader and didn't go to the public library, and I didn't read the Scottish newspapers. I got the news from Roscoff in Brittany and sometimes I read the local paper there, the *Télégramme*. Then sometimes on a Friday or Saturday evening I met with some of the other Onion Johnnies in Leith. It wasn't a club, it was just informal, everyone did his own thing, we just met as friends, as Onion Johnnies. Sometimes I worked on a Saturday afternoon, but sometimes I went then to the football, well, to Hibs at Easter Road. I liked to see football. Perhaps I was a Hibs supporter. I think I went once to see Hearts at Tynecastle, too. But I went to Easter Road, oh, only two or three times a year. It was at the time when Hibs had a good team, with Gordon Smith, Reilly, Johnstone.[20]

Onion Johnnies

Sometimes I went to the cinema – the Cameo at Tollcross – to see French films. Maybe two or three times I went there. I didn't go with any friends, I just went alone. It was common for Onion Johnnies in Leith to go to the cinema like that.

Well, I stopped working as an Onion Johnny at Leith in 1971. I was 46 years old then. I had been a Johnny there for 22 years – and one month before the war in 1939! By 1971 I was on my own. My father died at the age of 69 in September 1955 in Edinburgh Royal Infirmary. He is buried in Mount Vernon cemetery in Edinburgh. In later years my mother just remained at Roscoff and didn't return to Leith. So for my last four years as a Johnny I was on my own in Leith. By then my mother needed my support at Roscoff. There was also the question of my pension. If I stayed on in Leith working every season as an Onion Johnny I would have suffered a loss of some of my pension. So in 1971 I went back home to Brittany and worked there until I retired.

Ah, I had regrets about giving up work as an Onion Johnny at Leith. But I don't have regrets about spending 22 years as a Johnny there. I had good times in Scotland. I look back on those years with happy feelings. Scotland is a nice country and the people are very good. Well, the first years after I left Leith I kept in touch with some of my old customers, but not now. It's a long time ago and some of my old friends there have passed on.

The work of an Onion Johnny was very hard. When you went over to Britain it was in order to make a living for yourself. In Brittany, at Roscoff and St Pol de Léon, between August and December was a time of unemployment. If you were only a worker you had to make a living as best you could. There was no other choice open to you.

If I went back now to Leith and Edinburgh I'd look for an easier job than selling onions!

EUGÈNE GUYADER

My father, who was born in 1883, had a little farm at Roscoff in Brittany. It was a very small farm – oh, about one hectare or two-and-a-half acres, it was like a big garden, and he farmed it himself. He used to work his little farm but he used to go to England, too, as an Onion Johnny. He worked on his farm from about Christmas until the middle of July, then he went to England to work as an Onion Johnny and he used to stay there till Christmas. He came home for Christmas. He always came home for Christmas.

My father was eleven years old when he first went to England to sell onions. That was in 1894. He went to Torquay. I have a photograph that shows my father on board an onion ship at Torquay. So Torquay was his base and he worked all round Torquay selling onions. He never worked in Scotland or anywhere else in England, just at Torquay.

He worked every year at Torquay from 1894 until he went to do his military service in the French army about 1900. After that, he went back again to Torquay between July and Christmas and worked his farm from Christmas till July. Then he was called up as soon as the 1914–18 War broke out and he fought in France in the infantry. He was only slightly wounded but of his five brothers two were killed in the war.

My father lost his wife, too, when he was in the war. After his first wife died and left him with a daughter to bring up he married again. I am the oldest of three sons of his second marriage. So I had two younger brothers and an older half-sister.

Onion Johnnies

After the 1914–18 war my father started to go again to Torquay about 1920 to sell onions. He worked there every year doing that until the Second World War started in 1939. He went back to France then but he didn't return to England after the Second War. He died in December 1948 at the age of 65. I was working in Torquay myself when he died and I couldn't get back to Roscoff to attend his funeral. It was sad, but that was in the nature of the job.

I didn't know my grandfather Guyader, my father's father. I was only four or five years old when he died. But grandfather Guyader was an Onion Johnny, too. As far as I know he didn't ever work in Scotland but I suppose he did work in England, too, like my father. I don't know where in England my grandfather had been. But he must have first gone to work there as an Onion Johnny maybe in the 1870s, maybe round about the time of the Franco-Prussian War. I remember my grandmother Guyader very well, my father's mother. She was 95 when she died. And my father's brother, my Uncle Thomas, he, too, was 95 when he died. He was an Onion Johnny like my father and my grandfather Guyader. Uncle Thomas worked selling onions at Preston in Lancashire.

My mother was young when she died. She died at the age of 53. Before she got married – she was my father's second wife – she worked in the fields. Her father, who was also my godparent, had a small farm at Roscoff and until she got married to my father my mother worked on her father's farm. I was only eight when her father died so I didn't really know him much. He was never an Onion Johnny. I remember my grandmother, my mother's mother, but I don't know what she did for a living when she was a girl.

Then my mother's brother was an Onion Johnny, too. I have a photograph that shows him as well on board an onion boat at Torquay. And then my father's sister-in-law and her husband they used to go to Kirkcaldy in Fife to sell onions. One of my brothers was an Onion Johnny with me. So quite a number of members of my family were Onion Johnnies. But I don't know if my great-grandfather Guyader was an Onion Johnny: I can't go as far back in the family as that.

I think it was from Santec, a village about 3½ miles west along the coast from Roscoff, or between Roscoff and Santec, that the earliest Onion Johnnies left to work in England in 1828.

Well, I was born on 9 March 1922 in Roscoff, not far from the house where I live now. When I was about three or four years old I began at school, the Ecole Sainte Barbe. Then when I was eight I went to a second school – it had a name, only I don't remember now what it was. Anyway it was the school pupils went to once they reached the age of eight or nine. I liked the school but I don't remember very much about it. I liked arithmetic a little and was quite good at it – maybe it came in useful later on for counting the onions I sold as a Johnny! But, oh, I was young when I began at school and I was still young when I finished. Because I was the oldest boy in our family, I left school when I was twelve years old. That was in 1934. As I say, I liked the school – but I liked better to go out and work!

So that was the first year I went to work selling onions in England at Torquay, 1934. That was my first job. I wanted to go. I didn't have any ambitions to do anything else, like becoming a seaman or a fisherman or a railwayman. I just thought that as the oldest boy in the family I would like to help my parents, to help the family income, to make some money.

My father was the boss, the *patron*. There were nine of us working with my father at Torquay. The first time I went, in 1934, we were all nine or ten of us in the boat that took the onions from Roscoff to Torquay. It was small, 20 or 25 tons, like a fishing boat. As the boss it was my father who arranged for the cargo of onions to be taken over to Torquay. So the workers and the onions went together from Roscoff. Oh, there were so many boats that were going to England, and we all left about the same time – in the middle of July.

My mother and my brothers and half-sister came down to the harbour to see us off. My mother was weeping a bit when we set sail. Well, I was young, you see, I was twelve. Oh, I was very seasick on that first voyage. It took between 16 and 24 hours from Roscoff – a long way. Sometimes the sea was a bit rough, though it was in the summer and the weather was sometimes very nice. But the boat had no motor – it was a sailing boat.

At Torquay my father had an old stable as a base. The men, the Onion Johnnies, lived there and the onions were stored and strung there. The men all slept in one room, in a row, like herrings or sardines! But they all had a bed each. I had a bed to myself. My father, as the boss or *patron*, was at the end of the row. I wasn't next to my father but further down the row somewhere. I didn't feel anxious about being separated from him.

I was the youngest there. Then there was another lad who was maybe fourteen or fifteen. Then the other eight or so were older. The man who strung the onions in the stable was maybe thirty or forty years old. My father was the oldest. At that time, 1934, he would be about 51. Then there was another older man, though not as old as my father, who came from Santec. The other Onion Johnnies there were maybe aged from seventeen or eighteeen upwards.

Well, I found the first year at Torquay was very difficult. I said to myself, 'I won't come back. It's too hard.' It was very hard. But I did go back and I liked it afterwards.

That first year I was stringing the onions in the old stable. I went selling the onions only on Saturdays. Oh, the selling was difficult at the beginning. I didn't speak English at all. I could say 'Yes' and 'No'. My father didn't teach me very much English. But I soon learned to ask customers for a 'Penny for myself?'! I soon learned that English! People would give me a penny then. I didn't get many pennies to begin with as I was selling the onions only on Saturdays. But I used to go to the same places so people began to know me, and I suppose as I was only a boy of twelve they would feel sorry for me. So by a Saturday evening that first year I would have a few pennies for myself. I gave all those pennies to my father. Sometimes I kept tuppence a week. My father didn't mind that. With my tuppence I bought chocolates – that was my weakness! I didn't smoke, not before the 1939–45 War. I only started to smoke when I went to England after the war but I never became a heavy smoker and it's a long time ago since I smoked at all.

At the end of that first onion season in 1934, when we came back home to Roscoff, my father as the boss or *patron* gave whatever I had earned to my mother. I never saw or touched that money. It was only later on, when I was maybe fourteen, fifteen or sixteen, that he began to pay me whatever wage or salary I had earned. I don't remember very well now what the wage was that I received. The money then was not the same as it is now. What I do remember was that my pay wasn't very much! I didn't have a big salary at the end of the season to come home with! But once I was back home my mother would give me something on Sundays to go to the pictures with, you know.

As I say, I found that first year at Torquay really quite difficult. At the beginning I felt homesick. I'd never been away from home before and I was only twelve. The others at the old stable were older, or a lot older, than me. It was really the weight of the onions that was the problem. Torquay is really hilly. So going up and down hills made the job of selling the onions more difficult. And the first year I had to carry a pole or baton over my shoulder, with onions hanging from it. I didn't get many strings to carry on the baton, maybe only four or five, because I was only twelve years old.

But I had a bicycle the second year. My father gave me it. It was an English bicycle – a Raleigh. It was a good bicycle. It was very good for carrying the onions. And I had more then to carry! Each year as I got older and stronger my father gave me more onions to carry on it. But really every year we went the work became easier for me.

In Torquay before the 1939–45 War there were five separate companies of Onion Johnnies. My father's was only one of the five. So there were nearly 40 or 50 Onion Johnnies selling onions all around Torquay. Some of them even then before the war had a car and they were able to travel quite far with their onions.

There was strong competition at Torquay then between the companies of Johnnies. I remember some days I would go to a house about ten o'clock in the morning and the customer would say, 'Oh, there's been two Onion Johnnies here already this morning!' So it wasn't easy to sell the onions, it really was not very easy. Some days you wouldn't make or take in much money. But you never came back with your onions unsold, oh, no. You had to stay till you finished. Sometimes it was nine or half-past nine o'clock at night before you finished.

The working day began about seven o'clock. You rose from bed and had some *petit déjeuner*, breakfast, of coffee and bread. Then I would go with some onions about 7.30 or 8 o'clock, sometimes 8.30, and come back for dinner. My father said to me once: 'One o'clock, two o'clock, come home and get something to eat.' So I would sell onions till maybe two o'clock and then come back to the old stable again and have something to eat, then get another load of onions and go back out and sell them. But I didn't come back until they were finished, sold.

Oh, some days it was very difficult. But I don't think I ever came back with onions unsold, I don't think so, even if that meant working on till dark in winter. Oh, it was quite a hard life – long hours.

Then I had my main meal in the evening after work. It was my father who cooked the meal. He was a good cook. He cooked for everyone, all nine or ten of us. Some of the Johnnies went out in the morning and didn't come back till night, others went out in the morning and, if they sold their onions, came back for something to eat at lunchtime and then went back out again in the afternoon to sell more. But there wasn't a cooked meal for them at the old stable in the middle of the day. It was just a piece of bread or sandwich or something light like that.

Our clients sometimes asked us if we wanted something to eat and a cup o' tea. In some places we were offered some cake. People were quite kind in that way. There's good and bad people everywhere. We had very good people.

In the evening when my father cooked the meal it was soup first. Then we had steak, a beef steak each, *pommes de terre* - potatoes, *et les autres légumes* - other vegetables. The other vegetables we ate included onions! I don't eat them now, not much anyway. But the food was good.

At Torquay besides the onions we sold garlic and shallots. That was all, not cauliflower or cabbages or any other vegetables, just those three. But the main one of course was the onions.

The onions all came from around Roscoff and district and further up – a 15 or 20-kilometre radius around Roscoff. They were pink, reddish onions and were known as *oignons rosés*. Oh, they were good quality. Nowadays we put a chemical of some sort on them to preserve them better, so they keep better now than in those days. But, oh, they were good onions – otherwise it would have been more difficult to sell them in Torquay, because people in Torquay had gardens with plenty of their own onions growing in them. But the Torquay onions were not as good as the Roscoff ones.

There were plenty of hotels in Torquay, too. We used to sell our onions there – not the big hotels but the small hotels. I had some restaurants I used to sell them to there as well. But most of our clients were just ordinary people living in houses, rather than hotels, restaurants or cafes. One man at Torquay whom I knew when I was twelve years old is still alive in his late 80s. He was a garage mechanic at Torquay and he actually married a Breton woman from Santec. His wife died a few years ago but I still see him here at Roscoff sometimes.

Every year, when I came back home to Roscoff at Christmas, I worked on my father's small farm there until we went away again in July back to Torquay. I never worked for other farmers, just my father. He grew vegetables on the farm – onions, shallots, garlic, potatoes, cabbages. But it was only the first three that we sold at Torquay.

Well, I worked every season at Torquay from July till Christmas from 1934 until the Second World War started in September 1939. By that time I was seventeen and there were two other younger Johnnies there about my own age. The Johnnies who were old enough to go to the war left then of course for France. But we stayed on at Torquay for a couple of months to finish the onions and because we were too young for military service. We left Torquay in November that year, and sailed from Southampton to St Malo, zig-zagging as we went across the English Channel in order to avoid German submarines. But there were no submarine attacks and we got home safely.

I worked then near home at Roscoff on a farm where there were two women who had the farm. The man who was working for them had to leave and go off to the war. I went to work there in his place. The farm was more or less next door to my own home and I knew the people there very well. I stayed working there there till 1944.

It was then that the gendarmes – not the Germans – came to my home. They asked where I was. They said I had to go to Germany to work. Of course, though I wasn't at home when

they came I wasn't very far away – working on the neighbouring farm! So I decided I wasn't going to Germany and
that I would join the Maquis. So I went to the Maquis in May
or June 1944, just about the same time as the Allied landings
in Normandy on D-Day.[21]

When I joined the Maquis I went to Roscoff first then
further up. The Germans were trying to find where we were,
so then the Maquis sent me to the war in Lorient, *La Poche de
Lorient*, over 100 kilometres or about 75 miles south-east of
Roscoff, on the coast of the Bay of Biscay. I suppose they
thought it would be too dangerous for me to remain around
Roscoff where I was known. I learned to fire weapons – rifles
and machine guns and all that. To tell you the truth I didn't
take part in very much fighting against the Germans. I was a
bit late going to the Maquis, you see. But I did take part in
some fighting around Lorient, where four in my company of
the Maquis were killed in the fighting. The Americans came,
however, and the Germans were encircled and they surren-
dered then. I was there at that time.

Then from the Maquis I went into the French army, the
infantry, later in 1944 and I went to Germany with the army. I
was in the army for nearly two years, nearly a year of that
time in Germany. I came home from the army in May 1946.

I went back then to work on the neighbour's farm again,
but only for about a year. Then I started to go back to
England, to Torquay again, as an Onion Johnny in 1947. So I
worked selling onions again in Torquay for about ten years
until 1957. Things were different at Torquay after the war.
There were then only two companies of Onion Johnnies. In
our company there were only four of us. It wasn't so good.
There were less than a dozen Johnnies altogether at Torquay
when, before the war, there had been about 40 or 50. As I've
said, my father, like the other older Johnnies, didn't return to
Torquay after the war and in fact he died in 1948. On the
other hand, there was less competition at Torquay for us than

there had been before the war. So we sold a lot of onions – more than before the war.

In those years between 1947 and 1957 we worked as before: six months in England at Torquay and the other six months at St Pol de Léon near Roscoff. But at St Pol we didn't work in the fields, as I had done in earlier years, we worked in a local vegetable factory. We prepared vegetables – cauliflowers, cabbages, everything – cleaned them, packed them in boxes, and lorries or trains came and took them away all over France. So that was my job in the months between January and July.

In the vegetable factory it wasn't then 35 hours a week like now. I used sometimes to work there 60 hours a week – including Saturday all day – so it was six days a week. It was only in the later four or five years there we got a half-day off. Oh, it was hard work. But they told me then, 'It would be better for you to stay working here in the factory the whole year for ten years, instead of just working here for six months in the year.' What they meant was that my state pension would be affected and I would lose out eventually on it if I didn't work all year round in France for so many years in order to qualify for a full pension.

Then in 1957 my wife and I lost our son. He was ten years old. That year I stayed at home in Roscoff and didn't go to Torquay. Afterwards my younger brother, who had been working as an Onion Johnny in Glasgow since about 1950, said to me, 'Why don't you come with me to Glasgow?' So I went with him, and later on my wife joined me there.

My brother knew Glasgow very well by then. Our base in Glasgow was in Argyle Street at the beginning. I changed bases two or three times there. I only stayed in Argyle Street three years, I think. I don't remember the names of all the other streets where I stayed. Compton Place – a garage – was one.

In Argyle Street it was a small shop that was our base for

the onions and where we lived. The shop was maybe about 24 feet by 30 feet in size. There were four of us – my brother and myself and two other Onion Johnnies. We slept at the back of the shop. We had a bed each – well, it was bunks, two sets of bunks, one bunk on top of the other. I slept in the bunk above my brother.

The shop in Argyle Street had electric light all right but I had to go to the laundry to wash my clothes, although we could wash ourselves in the shop and could have a bath or a shower there. There was a flush toilet, too.

Our routine in Glasgow was much the same as it had been at Torquay. When we got up in the morning and when we set off with our onions depended on where we were going. We sold onions in Glasgow but also all around Glasgow, as far away as Hamilton, Motherwell, Blantyre, Carluke, Lanark, Stirling – a nice place, Falkirk, Kilsyth, Bathgate. At the beginning I went to Perth, too, and to Kirkcaldy. My brother knew Kirkcaldy because before he started working in Glasgow he had worked in Kirkcaldy with my brother-in-law. But after a time we decided it was no use to go so far from Glasgow as Perth or Kirkcaldy, because we had plenty of customers all around Glasgow itself.

But one important difference between Torquay and Glasgow was that at Glasgow from about 1960 I had a van. That meant we could go further afield. We put our bicycles in the van and my brother and me went off in the van. We parked the van some place, got out our cycles loaded with onions and went round our clients on them. When we'd sold those onions we came back to the van for more, loaded them up again, and set off again on the bikes. We went about once a month with onions to those various towns around Glasgow. With the van it was easy going. Before I got the van I went sometimes by train with my bike loaded with onions.

In Bathgate I had a good client who became a friend. He was a coal miner and his wife was a good woman. Unfortunately, the man died and his wife and their daughter emigrated to Australia.

By that time, the early 1960s, there were fewer Onion Johnnies in and around Glasgow. So competition was not so strong. In fact, two or three years before we finished there was only us two, my brother and me, around Motherwell, to which we had moved from Glasgow. By that time, of course, my wife had come over from Roscoff and joined us. Sometimes my brother and my wife stayed at the base, stringing the onions. So I was the only one who was going round selling them.

My brother didn't like it much in Glasgow. He found the city too noisy and dirty. There was a man I knew very well, Mr MacGregor, a customer, and he offered us the use of an old mill he owned at Motherwell. My brother was glad to go there, as I was. Oh, it was really nice at the old mill at Motherwell. It was a really good base for us. There was everything there we needed. We moved our base from Glasgow to Motherwell in 1965. The last six years I worked in Scotland the base was at the old mill in Motherwell. We had plenty of room there, plenty of space. The onions were stored in a separate room downstairs and my wife and I had a room to ourselves to live in, and so did my brother. My brother wasn't married, he was a bachelor.

Our move from Glasgow to Motherwell didn't change the area that we sold onions in. It was much the same as before – Glasgow and all round about it: Hamilton, Motherwell, Lanark, Carluke, Stirling. We stayed the same, and we continued to use the van as well as the bikes.

We found that people in Glasgow – not all maybe, but most – were generally friendly toward us when we came with our onions. Sometimes there was someone who was rude, who maybe said, 'I don't want any onions!' and shut the door on us – but it didn't happen often. There were some good, really good people, quite kindly. I liked Glasgow and Glasgow people. I found most people in Glasgow were really friendly. Every day I went to customers there I was offered a cup of tea in some places – every day.

And I remember in Lanark there was a woman who was really good. 'When you come with your onions,' she said, 'go and see your other customers and I'll make your tea ready.' There were other customers near her house, you see. And when I came back to her house a cup o' tea was ready and cake. She was really good. But I can't remember her name. She used to write to my wife and me in Roscoff until she died.

So there were several people who asked me in from time to time for cups o' tea or gave me sandwiches or cake or something like that to eat.

As the years passed, first at Glasgow then at Motherwell, the sale of our onions was increasing. It wasn't such a struggle as it had been in the early years at Torquay. Oh, it was better, easier, much easier. There were fewer Johnnies, less competition, and we had plenty of customers. We spent all those years building up our customers. When we were in Glasgow, even before my wife joined us there, we stayed there over Christmas and didn't go home then.

By 1971 I had been working as an Onion Johnny for 37 years, minus the years of the 1939–45 War, when I had been at home in Roscoff, or in the French army until 1946 or for a year or so after that working on our neighbour's farm. But, as I've said, when after the war I was working in the vegetable factory they said, 'It would really be better for you to stay home to make sure you qualify for your full state pension.'

It wasn't easy for me to give up being an Onion Johnny in Scotland. I liked the work and I liked the people there. I regretted really having to give it up. Oh, there were some tears! But it was the only thing I could do in order to get my pension. Of course I was torn. It wasn't easy after a lifetime of hard work to say goodbye to my customers. One or two of them were weeping as well!

Onion Johnnies

My wife liked the work in Scotland as well after she went there. She was pleased, of course, when I decided to retire and go back to live in France. She was pleased for me.

My brother didn't give up being an Onion Johnny at the same time as me. He carried on working with another man, who did the stringing of the onions. But my brother moved from Motherwell to Leith when I left to go home to France for good. He worked at Leith for about three or four years after that.

Well, it's almost as long now since I gave up being an Onion Johnny as it was that I worked as one. Looking back now on all my years as a Johnny, first at Torquay, then in Scotland at Glasgow and Motherwell, I'm glad to have been one really, oh, yes. It was a very good experience. I saw more of the world – Torquay, Glasgow, Motherwell, Bathgate, and all those other places I went to to sell the *oignons rosés* of Roscoff.

Onion Johnnies on board a sailing ship that brought them and their onions to work at Torquay c.1920s. Eugène Guyader's father is third from the left, with pipe and wearing a cap.

Eugène Guyader as a boy (right), c.1930, with his father, who was also an Onion Johnny but based at Torquay in Devon.

Anna Gourlet, an 'Onion Jenny', who first came at the age of 11 from Brittany to work with her parents as onion sellers at Leith, is shown here with her loaded bicycle in the later 1930s.

Eugène Guyader, who had worked as an Onion Johnny at Torquay before the 1939-45 War, moved his base to Glasgow in the later 1950s.

The mill at Motherwell, where Eugène Guyader, his wife and his brother were based as onion sellers from 1965 until 1971.

An Onion Johnny, with onions carried on a baton on his shoulder, makes a substantial sale to a customer at Inveresk, Musselburgh, in 1931. *Courtesy of East Lothian Libraries.*

Claude Quimerch (centre), who began working as an Onion Johnny in Glasgow about 1950, pictured here in 1966 with Claude Corrie (left) and Pierre Tanguy at their base in the city at 81 Kingston Street. 'Wee Claude' Corrie, born at Roscoff in Brittany in 1908, had begun work at age 12 as an Onion Johnny at Leith but later moved to Glasgow.

Onion Johnnies stringing onions at their base in Dundee in December 1965. The brothers Pierre and Henri Tanguy are on the right of the picture. *Courtesy of D.C. Thomson & Co. Ltd. Dundee.*

One of the Dundee Onion Johnnies with his heavily loaded bicycle in 1965. *Courtesy of D.C. Thomson & Co. Ltd, Dundee.*

Guy Le Bihan with two of his customers in the West of Scotland.

Guy Le Bihan (right), whose base was at Ayr from 1957 until 1978, and a fellow Onion Johnny with the van in which they daily transported their onions and their bicycles.

Guy Le Bihan (left) and a fellow Onion Johnny outside their base at Ayr.

Jean Milin, who first arrived in Scotland in 1929 from Brittany by sailing boat to sell onions as a boy aged 12 during his school holidays, became a year later a full-time Onion Johnny at Leith, based in Quality Street. This photograph, taken in 1930, shows Jean Milin, aged 13, with a heavy load of onions carried on a baton over his shoulder.

Jean Milin with his bicycle and onions in front of his garden and two-storeyed house at Plouescat in Brittany in 1994.

CLAUDE QUIMERCH

My father was an Onion Johnny, too, and until 1930 he used to go to Southampton to sell onions. He had started working as a Johnny in Southampton just before he was thirteen years old. He was born about 1897 and started working at Southampton about 1910, just before the First World War. He worked there with a big company of Onion Johnnies – about thirty or forty of them. At that time he worked during the onion-selling season for four or five months, then he came back home for Christmas and New Year.

My father fought in the 1914–18 War. He was the fifth of six brothers to go to the war. One of his brothers was killed in 1916 at Verdun.

My father while he was an Onion Johnny until 1930 always had a small farm in Brittany at Santec, on the coast, about five kilometres west of Roscoff. His father, my grandfather Quimerch, well, he was just a farmer, I think. I don't think he was an Onion Johnny, I never heard that. It was a small farm – too small to make a living out of it: only about half a dozen acres.

My father stopped working as an Onion Johnny in 1930 after twenty years. He gave up the farm then, too, and bought a lorry and he was going round the markets in Brittany at Guingamp, about 80 kilometres south-east of Santec, and at Saint Brieuc, another 35 kilometres beyond Guingamp. There was a market in Saint Brieuc on Wednesdays and Saturdays, and Guingamp market was on a Friday.

My father married twice. I was the only child of his first

marriage. I was born on 17 January 1923. I never knew my mother. I was only fourteen months old when she died from tuberculosis.

It was very difficult for my father. So he married again, and he had another five children, my step-brothers and step-sisters.

I was seven years old before I started the elementary school at Santec. Before then, because my mother had died of tuberculosis, I had to go to a sanatorium and have tests. I remember the sanatorium was in a big house. So I was seven when I started school.

I went for five years to the school at Santec and then when I was about 12 years old I went to a college at Morlaix, about 25 kilometres from Santec. I lived in at the college at Morlaix. It was a residential college and I had a room and a bed to myself there. I was there for four years until I was 16. At the college at Morlaix I studied English, Latin and Greek for four years. I was interested in languages so I also began to learn German and Spanish.

My ambition was to join the French navy. To be an officer in the navy you had to be good at mathematics and English. And I was good at English and mathematics.

Then in 1938 my father became ill. I was 16. That was the finish for me at the college at Morlaix. I had to leave and go home to work. I was disappointed of course at having to give up the college and my ambition to become an officer in the navy. But I was needed at home. My step-brothers and sisters were all younger or much younger than me.

When the war started in 1939 there was a new law came in that you could drive when you were sixteen. Before then the minimum age was 18 – and 21 for driving heavy vehicles. So I passed a test for driving when I was 16½. My first job was to drive my father's lorry to the markets, where since 1930 he had been a merchant, buying and selling.

Then in 1940, on the 1st of May, just before the Germans

arrived in France, my father died. He was only 43. I was then the only one in our family who was working and earning money. I had to earn money to help my stepmother and the family. She had to remain at home to look after the children. The youngest was only about 15 months old when my father died, and the twins were only three years old.

After the Germans arrived in France in 1940 I was allowed by them still to go with the lorry to Guincamp and Saint Brieuc. But because those places were in the Côtes-du-Nord, a different *département* of Brittany from where I lived at Santec, I was allowed to do that only for six months. Then that was it. I wasn't allowed any longer to go outside our own *département*, which was Finistère. Then after that I wasn't allowed to go with the lorry outside the area around Morlaix, so I couldn't even go to Brest or Quimper, although they were in the *département* of Finistère, too.

So then I changed my job from going with vegetables in the lorry to the markets, to becoming a wood merchant with the lorry and delivering wood to people for their fires. That was quite a change for me. But it was good enough, because I could go with the lorry about 35 or 40 kilometres around Santec out into the country with the wood for fires. The farms I went to with wood you could get butter, eggs, and grain – corn and barley. I didn't need to get vegetables from the farms – I had them at home. With the barley I used to make coffee – barley coffee. It wasn't very good coffee! But we had to make do with it during the German occupation.

So I was driving the lorry as a wood merchant's lorry. I didn't cut down trees myself. I just bought wood that was already cut down and sawn up. I transported it around the district. I took it to bakers, for instance, for baking their bread with. It was difficult for them to get coke or coal.

Then, of course, there were problems in getting petrol. We were only allowed 20 litres – about four gallons – a month. So after that we had to use *gazogène*, gas from wood, and you had a big balloon thing on the lorry for the *gazogène*. Oh, times were difficult! And my stepmother couldn't go out to work, of course, because she had my five young step-brothers and sisters to look after at home. So I was still the only one in the family working and earning some money.

In November 1943 the *garde champêtre*, the rural policeman at Santec, came one day when I was changing my *gazogène* for the lorry and handed me these papers. I had been called up to work in Germany! I told him I was looking for some paper for my *gazogène* – and I set fire to the call-up papers! Well, I was lucky, because about eight days later I was driving the lorry from Morlaix to Santec when it broke down. The *gazogène* wasn't working properly, it wasn't getting enough air to pass through. Sometimes you had cinders or clinkers, and when I was trying to sort things I hurt my arm. I had been working away at repairing things for some time and by then it was after ten o'clock at night. There was a curfew and you had to be home by ten o'clock. Two Germans arrived then: '*Allez – Kommandantur!*' So I had to follow them to the Kommandantur, the German headquarters. I had a friend with me from Plouigneau, near Morlaix. When the Germans asked me, 'What have you got in your pockets?', I was glad I didn't have my call-up papers to Germany that I'd set fire to. It was a good job I'd burned them!

But I was lucky again, because I wasn't again called up to go to Germany. All the men who were born in 1922 were called up by the Germans. There were 43 of us born in 1923 – -but only three of us were actually called up. The two others were fishermen – so they were excused. I was the third – but I had burned the papers and didn't go and I wasn't called on again! So nobody from Santec who was born in 1923 actually went to Germany.

After D-Day in Normandy in June 1944 I was driving the lorry in Morlaix with five bags of new potatoes and was also going to pick up a load of wood when I was stopped near the

Hotel de Ville by the Germans: 'We want your lorry.' So that was my lorry requisitioned by the Germans. That finished my lorry and wood business.

Well, then I was told to drive the lorry to Crozon, Kelgrouque, away on the west coast of Brittany, near Brest. I had to leave the lorry there and walk all the way back home to Santec – 110 kilometres, about 66 miles.

But I wasn't alone. I had two friends with me. Well, after we left the lorry we had walked about 20 kilometres towards home when we saw another lorry coming. By this time it was night – about half-past eleven – and we had to cross a bridge between Crozon and Daoulas. The Germans were there at the bridge on guard, of course. We had a laissez-passer, a pass. So the Germans let the three of us past. The lorry we had seen coming was driven by a fellow who was in much the same line of work as me. But he was working for the Germans with his lorry. It was full of bags of peas. But he stopped and picked us up and gave us a lift about 30 kilometres to Daoulas. He was allowed to drive through the night because he was working for the Germans. He dropped us off near a farm. We saw some straw there and lay down in it for two or three hours to sleep.

Well, it was light again by about five or six o'clock in the morning. So we got up to start walking again towards home at Santec. One of my two friends who were with me was a big merchant. He used to send vegetables in boxes by train to Paris and Lille and, oh, everywhere. Well, he saw some of his own boxes at the farm as we set off. The Germans had sometimes commandeered some of his vegetables in their boxes. It seemed that the lorry driver with the bags of peas who had given us a lift had brought some of my friends' vegetable boxes to this place, too. Well, when somebody at the farm appeared my friend told him who he was and the man said, 'Oh, OK, OK.' So we got breakfast given us there at the farm. And after we had eaten it the lorry driver with the peas offered to bring us in his lorry to St Pol de Léon, just a few kilometres away from Santec. He had plenty of petrol for his lorry because he had to work for the Germans.

Well, we set off but we were stopped by the Germans at Landerneau when we were more than half way home. At Landerneau a German colonel demanded that the lorry driver take him to Landivisiau, which fortunately for us was on the road anyway to Santec, about 17 kilometres further on. So the driver and we other three were in the front of the lorry and the German colonel was alone in the back of it! We dropped the German colonel off at Landivisiau and we got back safely to St Pol de Léon and then home to Santec after that.

When in August 1944 the Americans arrived in Brittany to liberate it from the Germans, I was with the Americans there. One day we went to a field at Plouvien, near Brest. The field was full of French lorries, vans and cars that the Germans had requisitioned. They had abandoned them there. So we were in the middle of the field and all these vehicles, trying to get a lorry. The Germans were only, oh, 700 yards away from us, and the Americans about the same on the other side. We were in the middle! Well, I didn't find my own lorry there but we got another one. We got petrol for it from the Americans, who were blacks. We painted the Cross of Lorraine – De Gaulle – on the lorry.[22] Later on I found my own lorry again, though its engine wasn't working because there was no oil in it.

Then after the war I was, well, a vegetable merchant if you like but really I was working for a big merchant at St Pol de Léon. The big merchant brought empty vegetable boxes to me and I was filling the boxes with artichokes or cauliflowers, onions, carrots, all kinds of vegetables. I did that kind of work for about four or five years, until 1948 or 1949.

For two or three seasons after the war I was also working with sugar beet. The season was from the 1st of October until Christmas or New Year. It was only three months and the work was in a factory in the *département* of Seine et Marne, in the north of France. We stayed there, living at the factory. That sugar beet work was in the area of Pithiviers, Joinville, Meaux. There were plenty of sugar beet factories there. The factory I went to was at the other side of Paris, beyond Meaux, at a place called Lizy-sur-Ourcq. There were about sixty or seventy of us from Santec, Roscoff and St Pol de Léon in Brittany who went there to work. There were not many vegetables available just then in Brittany – so there was no work nearer home. I lived at the factory. It was a new experience for me.

In 1945 I got married. We had two daughters, one born in 1946, the other in 1953.

Then in 1949 or 1950 Jean Saout, who lived in St Pol de Léon and worked as an Onion Johnny *patron* or boss at Glasgow, and Hervé Prigent, his brother-in-law, came to see me. They asked me to go with them to Glasgow as their van driver. So that's how I started as an Onion Johnny.

We went by train to Glasgow. When we arrived in London I didn't know if we were in England or Paris! My first impression was the way people spoke English. They were speaking Cockney. I felt a dunce in English! I felt quite lost. Later I found they speak better English in Scotland than they do in England. It's clearer.

My first impressions of Glasgow was what a big city it was, and very industrial.

We were not in a good place in Glasgow. We were in Kingston, near the Gorbals. We were in a shop at 97 Kingston Street. Well, I started at No. 97 and I finished years later at No. 81 Kingston Street. And then the last two years I worked in Glasgow I was in Centre Street, near the fire station, about 200 yards from Kingston Street.

In Kingston Street our places were all shops. One of the shops I remember was a paper shop. It was No. 81 and that was the one we were in years later. In one corner of the street there was a bar, and at the other corner was a bank – Bank of Scotland. The paper shop was near the bank.

When we arrived at No. 97 Kingston Street when I began there in 1950 the shop was empty. But we had another shop in West Street, at the corner with the bank, and the onions were stored there. The onions were strung in the two shops, too. So the onions were stored in West Street, and we lived and did some of the stringing of the onions at No. 97 Kingston Street. We didn't store onions at No. 97 when I first went there because there were about eleven of us Onion Johnnies living there. There wasn't room to store onions as well!

There were really four *patrons* or bosses in our company in Glasgow: there was Jean Saout, his brother-in-law Hervé Prigent, and there were two brothers, André Chapalain and Joseph Chapalain. There were two men who were stringing the onions. And there were two sons of André Chapalain. I think there were eleven of us altogether there, seven of us were *ouvriers*, ordinary workers, Onion Johnnies, and the other four were the bosses.

The room at No. 97 where we all slept was maybe about thirty feet by forty feet. We had beds – well, bunks, in twos, one bunk above the other. We had water in the shop but no electricity at first. There was gas lighting. There was a toilet in the corridor. We shared the toilet with others. You see, there were two companies of Onion Johnnies. In another shop – I think it was No. 93 – there was another company with about seven or eight Johnnies. Their *patrons* or bosses were Franc Prigent, Claude Corrie, and Yvon Guyader. So they used the same toilet as us at No. 97. There wasn't a bath or shower: we had to go about 200 yards on to the Paisley Road to the public baths. I lived and worked at No. 97 Kingston Street for about ten years from 1950. Then I was at No. 81 for maybe three or four years, and the last two or three years I was an Onion Johnny in Glasgow I was in Centre Street.

Claude Quimerch

Although Jean Saout and his brother-in-law Hervé Prigent had asked me to go to Glasgow as their van driver, in fact at first we had no van. Chapalain, Prigent and the other *patrons* didn't then have enough money to buy a van. We had to wait a month and a half before a van was bought. So at first I had a bicycle to sell the onions from. In fact, I had a bike for ten seasons!

Well, the first day I went out in Glasgow to sell onions on the bike it was Fotheringay Road I went to. It wasn't far from Kingston Street. It was in Pollokshields, about two miles maybe from Kingston Street. So I had to do the apartments – tenements – in Fotheringay Road. And the first bunch of onions I sold was at the 74th door I knocked at or rang the bell at! There was nobody in at the first 73. They were all out working. But I didn't feel discouraged. It was my first day at selling.

At the bottom of the stair at each tenement there were six bells. I pushed the bell – well, I took all six at once and pushed them all! All of them rang. People were hanging out their windows or calling down the stair, 'Who's there?! Who's there?!' It didn't make me popular! Oh, some of them were quite angry. Anyway when one got the message the others were getting it, too!

But after that I found people in Glasgow were very, very friendly. In Brittany people used to say about Scotchmen they always had their pocket for money. But I found the contrary. For at Hallowe'en, instead of getting maybe £10 for a bag of onions we got £13 or £14, and at Christmas and New Year we got double payments. People paid us more than they need have done, to give us our Christmas and New Year.

I don't know how many times I was offered a cup o' tea from customers at their houses. I had to tell them, 'Oh, I'm just about finished, I'm just at the last door.' We didn't have time to drink tea – we had to sell the onions. But, oh, I was often asked to have a cup o' tea. I was invited into the house for it often. But usually I had to say, 'Thank you. But no thanks. I have no time.' But sometimes when I was too cold in the wintertime I took a cup o' tea from a customer. But often I had to refuse, because if I took too much tea I'd be running to the toilet!

And then one Christmas Day later on, when I was working with Claude Corrie, there was a customer who sent a taxi for us to take us to his house for a meal. Three of us Johnnies – Claude Corrie, myself, and another named Pierre Tanguy – went. The man was Mr Cameron, a customer and friend of Claude Corrie. Mr Cameron lived in Paisley Road in Glasgow. He was a surveyor. And at midnight that Christmas Day he got a taxi to take us back home again. I think Mr Cameron came with his sister to visit Claude Corrie in Brittany a few years ago.

I cannot remember anyone in Glasgow who was impolite or rude to me. No one ever shut their door in my face, never. People were friendly. One or two of my regular customers tried to speak to me in French. And I remember one customer who spoke Breton to me. He was a Scotsman and he was dropped by air in 1943 in the south of our *département* of Finistère in Brittany. He was parachuted in to work with the maquis as a kind of spy, an agent. When he was with the maquis in Brittany he was injured, he hurt his leg. After the war he went back to Scotland and I sold onions to him. He didn't live in Glasgow, he lived between Milngavie and Killearn. He came over once to Santec, where I live in Brittany, though I wasn't there at the time – I was in Scotland selling onions – and he took part in a ceremony to commemorate Canadian sailors who had been killed during the war in a boat that was sunk not far from Santec. Some of the dead men were buried in Santec.

But that was not the first Scotsman I remember who spoke Breton. There was another one who was a customer of Joseph Chapalain. He came once to our shop in Kingston

Street and spoke in Breton to the two Johnnies who were stringing the onions there.

Most of my customers were women, though, not men – the *femme de ménage*, the woman in charge of the household. I got on well with my customers and, as I say, I don't remember anybody who was impolite.

The van we had at Kingston Street in Glasgow held two or three tons of onions. So when we were selling onions outside Glasgow we would put the bikes in the van with the onions and once we arrived wherever we were going for that day we would take the bikes out the van, load them with the onions, and pedal off on them round the district. When we had finished selling the first lot, well, we came back to the van for another lot.

Glasgow was a big city. When we started in 1950 the population there was about a million. But, you see, there weren't enough customers for us in Glasgow! In Gorbals, for example, we weren't able to sell our onions. The people there'd got no money. I mean, Gorbals had many very poor people. And there was quite a lot of unemployment there. We needed to go where there was money. And then in Glasgow there were shops, vegetable shops, all around. So we had to go out more to the suburbs of Glasgow where people were better off, and then outside the city itself and away to other towns and places. There was much more money in places like Milngavie, Bearsden, Clarkston.

So we changed districts, to try to sell the onions. As I've said, the first place I went to in Glasgow to sell them when I arrived there in 1950 was Fotheringay Road. But I went later to a lot of other places. I've mentioned Milngavie, Bearsden, Clarkston, but I went also to Balfron, Dumbarton, Balloch, Alexandria. I was at Kilmarnock and Muirkirk in Ayrshire. In Lanarkshire I went to Motherwell, Carluke, Lanark. I was in Dumfries and Stranraer and Carlisle. These places I went to in the van, with the bikes inside it.

Sometimes we went to Campbeltown for a weekend or a

week, and to Lochgilphead. When we went to Campbeltown we left Glasgow on, say, Monday morning about six o'clock. We started to sell the onions in Inveraray, then we went down to Lochgilphead, Ardrishaig and Tarbert, and then to Campbeltown. We went to Machrihanish, too. Sometimes we went the other way, from Lochgilphead north to Oban, by Kilmartin and Carnasserie.

When we were at Campbeltown we slept in a house: a customer gave us accommodation there. He didn't charge us for the accommodation. We gave him some onions: onions for a'thing! An exchange! And we slept, too, in Lochgilphead – but in a hotel. That was more expensive. But the owner of the hotel was a customer for our onions. So we sold him some onions. In Oban we slept also in a hotel, a customer's hotel. There we paid, we paid. In Oban we saw an arena – the same as they had in Rome: McCaig's Folly. But we didn't sleep in that![23] I think I was only twice selling onions in Oban. We went there just at the beginning of the season in August because it was a market for sheep and plenty farmers came there. So instead of going from farm to farm in the countryside we sold the onions at Oban during the market days. Sometimes we had to sleep in the van, too, when we were in places away from Glasgow. So we moved through Argyll, selling the onions.

We also went to sell onions at Kilmarnock, Saltcoats, Largs, Wemyss Bay, Gourock, Greenock, Johnstone and Kilbarchan, as well as Paisley, Thornliebank and East Kilbride and, as I've already mentioned, Clarkston, Milngavie and Bearsden. In Thornliebank one customer was a Frenchman – a man from Alsace, who was married and lived in Thornliebank. When I started about 1950 or so to sell onions in East Kilbride it was about the same size as Santec in Brittany, it was no bigger, with several hundred inhabitants. That was all. Now East Kilbride's a big new town. And there they have no crossroads – just roundabouts, and you have roads for cycles and for pedestrians.

Claude Quimerch

We had regular rounds, every three or four weeks, to see the same customers. Sometimes the customers would buy the onions, sometimes they said, 'Sorry, we don't need them.' If they could use a bunch of onions every month or two months, fine. We went to Campbeltown every month.

As well as customers in houses we went to sell the onions to cafes and restaurants, and hotels. I remember the Central Hotel at the Central Station, and the St Enoch Hotel, and in Buchanan Street and all over. The hotels were good customers and bought a lot of onions. We did a delivery of onions to hotels on Saturday afternoons or Monday mornings. Italian cafes, too, bought quite a lot of onions – onions and garlic – from us.

I and the other Johnnies in our company at Kingston Street normally got up about six o'clock in the morning. We had some breakfast and then you went out to sell the onions maybe at seven o'clock or half-past seven, depending where you were going and which customers you had to see. You had customers that you did not get if you went to them after eight o'clock in the morning, because they were away to work. So they were customers you did find at home on Saturdays. Once you found them they told you you could come any day in the week – but come at half past-seven in the morning! So, you see, sometimes at half-past seven in the morning I was selling onions in Milngavie. Otherwise it was too late. On those mornings I was up at six o'clock. There was another Johnny and for him it was always half-past ten, or nearly eleven o'clock in the morning, before he went away to sell the onions. But it was ten o'clock or half-past ten at night before he came home. I was different: sometimes I had finished by one o'clock in the afternoon.

Every day was different. It depended on when the customers were at home to buy the onions. If they weren't going to be there, there was no point in going to their door. Sometimes you left the onions at the door and you got your money next time you went. It was safe to leave the onions like that. They were never stolen. You'd just leave the onions at the door. The customers always paid the next time you went to them. I trusted them and they trusted me.

So usually I would start work about seven or seven-thirty in the morning. But, as I say, it would vary from one day to another and one week to another. I worked on until about *midi, une heure*, midday or one o'clock, when I was working alone. Then I would eat some biscuits, a packet of biscuits – Rich Tea biscuits – and half-a-pound of grapes. Sometimes I had a packet of biscuits in my pocket when I went to customers and I gave some of the biscuits to the children. I didn't take bread or sandwiches with me to eat at midday, just biscuits and grapes.

I didn't take tea with me, I didn't have a thermos flask with tea. As I said, sometimes in wintertime we'd get a cup of tea from customers, though I had to refuse often, otherwise . . . ! But for something to drink at midday or one o'clock we went to a pub when there was one. In Milngavie there wasn't a pub at first, and it was years later before there was a place – a hotel – you could get a drink there. We drank beer, just a glass, a half-pint, of beer. So most days it was just a half-pint of beer, biscuits and grapes I had.

You didn't stop working at midday, unless you were going into a pub for a half-pint. I just carried on working and I ate the grapes and biscuits as I went round selling the onions.

Sometimes, as I say, I was finished working by one o'clock and went back to the shop. But when we went back to the shop we had work to do there. We had to separate the onions out for stringing. There was always work to do in the shop. You could go out again to sell more onions in the afternoon, you could do that. But the next morning there wouldn't be enough ready strung to sell. It was better stringing some in the afternoons and getting them ready for the next day.

So some days I finished maybe at one o'clock, but other

days I could be finished at eight or nine o'clock at night. Oh, it could be as late as nine o'clock sometimes. The hours varied from one day to another. You didn't work just from eight in the morning till five at night! The hours were very varied. And if you weren't selling the onions, you were in the shop stringing them. But when you finished selling them that day you went back to the shop and had a steak to eat!

You worked from Monday morning to Saturday evening. But on a Saturday we used to finish one hour earlier. Then on Sunday we worked from nine o'clock in the morning to one o'clock. That was normally every Sunday. Nearly every Sunday I went out with the van to get straw or rushes from the farms to make the strings for the onions.

The rushes made good strings for the bunches of onions. They were strong and better than straw. We went out about ten miles from Glasgow to near Milngavie to get the rushes. Oh, we never asked the farmers. We never paid the farmers for taking them. When you went and you saw the rushes, well, they were growing wild and there were plenty of them. We had a sickle or a knife to cut them. When we went for straw we paid the farmers for that.

On Sundays I didn't go to mass. I don't know if that was unusual for an Onion Johnny not to go to mass. The other Johnnies I worked with in Glasgow didn't go to the mass regularly on a Sunday. But I certainly didn't go when we were in Scotland. I didn't go to mass either at home in Santec. My wife and I were Catholics but not very devout. In Brittany it was the tradition that most people were devout Catholics, but not in our case. My wife and I were at mass one Sunday in October or November 1946, I don't remember which month it was. But there were elections on at the time, or a referendum. It was to be yes or no on the roll. And when we went to mass all we heard from the priest was about yes or no. We didn't want politics – so since then we haven't been at mass. We objected to the priest telling us whether to vote yes or no.

If I was going to the mass it was not to hear about politics or De Gaulle or yes or no. So I didn't go back![24]

As I've said, there was always work to be done. When you weren't selling the onions you were working in the shop stringing them, and on Sundays going out for rushes or straw. But on Sunday afternoons we played dominoes or cards. Then I played with a team of darts players. I was quite good at darts and I enjoyed that. Every Saturday night there was a darts championship from bar to bar. Our team was in West Street, but I don't remember what it was called.

I never went swimming or went for walks. Sometimes, not often, not regularly, I went to football matches. I went on the 1st of January, at New Year, to see Celtic and Rangers. Once I was at Rangers, the other year at Celtic. The way it was was that Celtic supporters were there, Rangers supporters were there, and ourselves – the Johnnies – were in the middle. At half-time the supporters started throwing cans of beer or flasks of whisky. Oh!

Once we went to see Nantes play Celtic. Three of us Onion Johnnies got our photograph taken and we got the players from Nantes to sign the back of the photograph for us. I think there were maybe 50,000 Celtic supporters at the match but us three Johnnies who went to watch were the only supporters for Nantes![25] I remember going to watch Queen's Park, Clyde, and Third Lanark playing. But mainly it was just Rangers and Celtic at New Year. Then we went to Hampden to see some international matches. I remember seeing Scotland and England, and Scotland and Hungary there.

At New Year we celebrated just among ourselves as Johnnies. But I remember once Claude Corrie and myself and the brother of Eugène Guyader, and another Johnny from Roscoff, went in the van to Edinburgh at New Year. I think we were invited to go to a Catholic club there, and we all played at cards.

*   *   *

Claude Quimerch

Between the onion-selling seasons in Scotland I was working as a driver at St Pol de Léon at home, driving vegetables. The first year I worked in Scotland I was back home in January. The second year I was back home on the 11th of November. It varied from one year to another. Some years I was back before the end of the year, in November or December. Other years it would be January, February or March. I remember one year – that was in 1963 – I was back at the end of January and it was a very hard winter. I was working for two months then with a spade, to bring water in! Then Jean Saout and I went back to Scotland again on the 4th of April and went back home again at the end of May, and then back to Scotland at the end of July. But that was unusual. Usually you left home to go to Scotland at the end of July or the beginning of August. That's when the onions were ready and the selling season was beginning. The Onion Johnnies always started to go to England, Scotland or Wales with the onions after the Pardon, the *Sainte Barbe*, Saint Barbara's Day. That was a Sunday and Monday in July.

Usually I went by train to Scotland. But when I went in April 1963 I went by boat from Roscoff to Portsmouth. We left Roscoff about half-past three or four o'clock in the morning and we reached Portsmouth at half-past seven at night. And it was snowing. So the boat was unloaded the day after. We got a lorry and put the onions on the lorry to go to Glasgow. In Scotland it was snow, snow, snow. I was there till the 21st of May and all the time it was snow. And when I came back home to Santec on the 24th of May I came to London, Dover-Calais. It was snowing in Dover and snowing in Calais! I remember, too, the first season I went to Scotland in 1950 the snow started on the 17th of September. Oh!

Sometimes when we went by train to Scotland it was normally from Roscoff to Paris, and then to Dieppe and Newhaven. But sometimes it was Boulogne-Folkestone or Calais-Dover. And sometimes it was St Malo-Southampton. The train journey from Roscoff to Paris took all night. We left Roscoff about eight o'clock at night, we changed trains at Morlaix and we arrived in Paris about five o'clock in the morning. And then of course from London to Glasgow by the train was another eight or nine hours, all night.

Sometimes I travelled alone to Scotland, sometimes there were other Johnnies with me. Sometimes we put garlic on the boat from Roscoff to Portsmouth. And once I went by train to Paris, Dieppe-Newhaven, and by train again to Portsmouth, and then I took the garlic to Glasgow by lorry. So that time I drove from Portsmouth to Glasgow.

About 1964 or 1965 Jean Saout retired from being an Onion Johnny, a *patron*, a boss. So I worked then with Claude Corrie – who had started work as an Onion Johnny when he was only 12 years old – and another Johnny, Pierre Tanguy, at No. 81 Kingston Street. There were just the three of us, and Pierre did the stringing. But after three or four years there all the shops were to be pulled down, *démolis*. And after that I went to Centre Street, next to Kingston Street. Claude Corrie was dead by then and I was with a different company of Johnnies.

I remained working in Scotland as an Onion Johnny until 1970. By then I had nobody to string the onions. The other Onion Johnnies had retired or had gone back home to Brittany for reasons of social security. Because I worked as a Johnny in Scotland for twenty years I lost about ten years on my state pension in France. So when I retired later on I had a smaller pension. But that was the reason I decided to stop working as an Onion Johnny in Scotland, and that was the reason the other Johnnies stopped, too. We couldn't afford to lose so much of our pension. When I went back home to Santec in 1970 I was working for another 14 years, then I retired in 1984.

Now when I look back on those 20 years I worked in Scotland as an Onion Johnny I sometimes wonder if I really was there! Time seems to have passed so quickly. It's already thirty years since I worked in Glasgow selling the onions. I lost part of my pension because I worked abroad, so in some ways I regret that part of things. Being an Onion Johnny was a hard life, a very hard life. But it would have been the same if I had been working at home in Brittany. Things were difficult there. From June to October in Brittany there was no work going at the big vegetable merchants. There was a wee bit of work with artichokes, just a wee bit, but nothing else. So you couldn't find work at home and that was why the Onion Johnnies had to travel so far from home. Some went to England, some to Scotland, some to Wales with the onions. Some men in Brittany had to wait till October to go and work for three months at the sugar beet, as I did some years after the war. So at least going to Scotland to work as an Onion Johnny gave you two or three months more work than you could find in Brittany.

As I say, being an Onion Johnny was a hard life. But it was even harder for my wife, because for the first four years I was a Johnny I didn't get paid my wages until the end of the season. So my wife had to live for six or seven months without any pay coming in. She felt like an abandoned wife! As I've mentioned, we had two girls, one born in 1946, four years before I became an Onion Johnny, and the other in 1953, two or three years after I first went to work in Glasgow. But my wife had no income during the onion-selling season. How she managed during those months for those four years is a mystery. We certainly didn't have plenty money! It was very hard, very, very hard. My wife didn't have a job because she had the girls to look after.

It's a long time ago and I can't remember exactly but I think at the end of my first season as an Onion Johnny in Scotland, when I went in July 1950 and came back in January 1951 I came back with about 125,000 francs for six months' work – which was about £125 then. There were about 1,000 francs to the pound at that time. And at the end of the next three seasons it was the same again – I was only paid at the end of the season. It was a hard life.

Madame Marie-Jo Quimerch

The first season my husband Claude was working as an Onion Johnny in Scotland I was without money and alone at home in Santec with my elder daughter, who was then four years old. Well, I got by by living on *bouillie*, a mixture of flour and milk. I put in some flour and some milk and mixed them together and we had that every day to eat. We simply had no money. I had no job. I had my daughter to look after. All the time Claude was in Scotland – six months – he wasn't paid. We survived on almost nothing. We ate almost nothing. There were no benefits at all paid us by the state, above all once Claude had gone to Scotland. There was absolutely nothing like that. Milk was our staple food. Oh, it was hard. My family did what they could to help us. My mother lived at Roscoff. But, well, I daren't tell her that I had no money, I daren't tell her that. Normally Claude and the other Johnnies signed a book and that was them hired for six months. Of course, you could ask the wives of the Johnnies' bosses – the bosses themselves were over in Scotland or England working and sending cheques to their wives. The wives had money, they had our money but they didn't give us any of it.

I remember I was expecting my second daughter. I waited for the postman because we were due a payment of benefit at three months, another at six months and another at eight months. I waited for the postman to come. I said, 'If at least I have my benefit payment!' But nothing came. The benefit came just when Claude came back with his money, then the benefit came too. At last I had some money! Oh, what a life!

It would have been nice if after the Johnnies had worked for a month they had been paid at least for a fortnight's work. But, oh, there was nothing. And you daren't go and ask for a payment because everybody around Santec would know you were the woman who had asked for money.

All the Johnnies and their wives and families were in the same state as us – except the *patrons*, the bosses and their wives. The bosses sent their wives cheques to buy food and all that. Oh, yes, oh, yes, it was hard.

Claude was 27 when he first went to work as an Onion Johnny in Scotland. He worked there for twenty years – or half-years. It was ten years altogether in half-years. All those years he went away twice and came back home twice. Oh, la, la, it was hard. Claude had good friends but we also had our pride. I couldn't, I wouldn't ask for money because one of the bosses – there were four or five of them – but one of them was a cousin and his wife was also a cousin. But I daren't ask for help because everybody would know about it. One of my friends said, 'But, Marie-Jo, you can't carry on like that.' Well, I did and I made it.

It was a sort of slavery for the families of the Johnnies. I used to take two or three spoonfuls of flour and added some milk to it, and even later on some sugar. People said, 'You'll not survive.' But I struggled on for the sake of our girls.

Claude found work again here. He was a driver, a lorry driver, between the onion-selling seasons. Sometimes he finished at three or four o'clock in the morning. Oh, it was hard.

JEAN-MARIE TANGUY

There were four generations of us Onion Johnnies in my family. My great-grandfather Tanguy, who must have been born about the 1840s or 1850s, went to Scotland – to Dundee – to sell onions. I never knew him and I don't know when he died. But I can remember my grandfather Tanguy. He was an old man when I remember him, too old then to go to Scotland any longer to sell onions. But he'd been there earlier on. He died when he was 86, in 1957. So he was born about 1870 or 1871.

My father Henri Tanguy was an Onion Johnny, too. He was born in Roscoff in Brittany on 3 May 1903, and he died when he was 77, in 1980. He spoke very good Scotch, my father. He always worked as an Onion Johnny in Dundee. He began selling onions in Scotland when he was very young, before the 1914–18 War. He was as well known in Scotland as he was at Roscoff. The Scots called him Harry Tanguy. My father worked in Scotland as an Onion Johnny for 53 years, and so did his brother Pierre. During the Second World War my father fought in the French army – the 41st infantry regiment. But he was very lucky, he wasn't wounded.

My father was also a farmer. He had a very small farm at Roscoff, only about two hectares – about five acres. On the farm he grew only vegetables – no grain. He grew onions, cauliflowers, artichokes, shallots, garlic, carrots, potatoes, cabbages – always vegetables, nothing else. The main vegetables he grew were the onions. After growing the onions he went to Dundee to sell them.

My mother before she married my father worked on her father's farm. They were wee farmers, no' big ones, just wee farmers – a few hectares. She helped her father on the farm. He grew onions, too, and he was an Onion Johnny as well. My mother, too, went to Dundee with my father before the 1939–45 War.

Well, I was born in 1929, on the 10th of December, at Roscoff. I had no brothers or sisters, I was just myself.

When I was five I started school at St Pol de Léon, at St Jean Baptiste school. But then when I was about six or seven in 1935 or 1936 I went for the first time to Dundee with my mother and father, and I went to school there for maybe one or two years. I can't remember now the name of the school in Dundee. I could speak a few words of English when I first went to Scotland. The school in Dundee wasn't difficult for me. I could understand what the teachers there were saying to me. Then after maybe a year or two years I came back to Roscoff again and went back to school at St Pol de Léon before the Second World War began in 1939. At school I liked all the subjects – mathematics, French, geography, I liked them all, and I got on well at school. But I didn't want to remain at school after the usual leaving age, which was fourteen then. So I was quite happy to leave in 1943 or 1944 when I was fourteen. I didn't have any particular ambitions as a boy, except to work on my father's farm and help my parents.

So when I left school I started work on my father's farm. I worked on the farm from then until I was 21, in 1951. Well, before then, when I was 20, I also did my military service in the French navy. There wasn't a choice of doing your military service either in the army or in the navy! It was usual for lads like me at Roscoff to go to the navy to do their service rather than the army. So I spent about fifteen months doing my service in the navy, and then I went back to help my father on the farm.

Onion Johnnies

At that time I had a boat and used to go out on the sea to harvest kelp. Once you got the kelp, it was dried on an island nearby – I've forgotten the name of the island. Once it was dry, the kelp was taken by boat to the land and then to the farm. You went out then with the tractor and spread the kelp as a manure in the fields The kelp was like a fertiliser.

Well, it was after I had done my service in the navy that I started to go to Scotland, to Dundee, with my father to sell onions. I would have gone to Scotland as an Onion Johnny as soon as I left school at fourteen. But I didn't go until I was 21 because, of course, when I left school the war was on. The Onion Johnnies didn't go to Britain for five or six years then. My father had begun to go back to Scotland – to Dundee – after the war, in 1947.

When we went to Dundee in 1951 we went on the train from Roscoff to Montparnasse station in Paris. It was four hours from Roscoff to Paris. We left Roscoff about five in the evening. Then from Montparnasse we took a taxi to St Lazare station on the other side of Paris. From St Lazare we went on the train again to Dieppe. That was two or three hours. From Dieppe on the ferry across the Channel to Newhaven was three and a half hours. From Newhaven we took a train to Victoria station in London. That was about two hours. Then a taxi to King's Cross station. From there we got another train to Dundee. That was a long journey – about ten hours, and quite tiring. We didn't have sleepers, we just sat in the carriage and dozed. We took our own food and some wine with us for the journey. That was the journey we made every year after that to Scotland, to Dundee.

We went always in July to Dundee and then I came home again at Christmas. But my father stayed on in Scotland till January. I travelled home alone at Christmas without him. But I didn't mind that when I was coming home. My mother was glad to see me. She wearied of being on her own at home.

Then I worked on my father's farm again from the end of the onion-selling season until we went back to Dundee again the following July.

In Dundee we lived in Dock Street, near the harbour. My father had been in Dock Street for a long time. He had a little shop there where he stored the onions and worked with them. He and his brother were there. My father employed me and he had six or seven other Onion Johnnies in the company. The other Johnnies came also from Roscoff or from St Pol de Léon, Santec and Sibiril, which was about six kilometres west of St Pol, but mainly from Roscoff. The others travelled with us on the train and ferry from Roscoff to Dundee.

Two of the Johnnies, Graal and Ezekiel, worked in the shop stringing the onions. To string a bunch of onions took, oh, just two or three minutes. There were about a dozen onions in a string. My father and I and the other Johnnies went out and sold the onions.

When I started first selling the onions in Dundee we used a baton to carry the onions. I used a baton for two or three years maybe. After that we used bicycles. It was easier with the bicycle than carrying the onions over your shoulder on a baton.

Before the war my father had used a motor bicycle with a sidecar. He put the onions in the sidecar. But if there was rain or snow it was no good. Everything got soaked. Then after the war he bought a van to take the onions out to sell, and the bikes were in the van, too.

At Dock Street we all slept in the shop with the onions. I didn't mind that. The onions – Roscoff onions – had a good smell! Yes, it was a nice smell.

At first when I began as a Johnny I went out with my father. My father went to one street and I went to another. Speaking English to the customers was difficult for me at first. My father told me what to say: 'You speak like that.' At first I rang the customer's bell: dddrrrrrrr, dddrrrrrrr. 'Do you want some onions, Missus, please?' 'Oh, yes, yes, yes.' But at first I didn't sell many onions! But soon I didn't find it was difficult.

Once I got a bicycle it was easier. We put the strings and bunches of onions on the bike and just went up this street and that street, selling them as we went. You went mainly to regular customers who had bought them from my father before – mainly to people we knew would buy the onions. We didn't go round every door trying to sell them. We went to the regular customers, who knew we were coming.

We went to a different place every day. Most of the customers we went to every three weeks. But at St Andrews we went every fifteen days. At Crieff or Forfar or Perth we went every three weeks. Three weeks was what our customers wanted.

The Scotch people, you know, wouldn't eat all the onions we had sold them the last time before three weeks were up: 'No eat. Plenty. No, no.' Three weeks meant 'Yes'. They liked to have three weeks to eat the onions. Scotch people don't eat onions like French people. We eat onions for soup, for everything – everything. But the Scotch don't eat so many onions.

We sold onions in Dundee but also in Forfar, Brechin, Montrose, Laurencekirk, Kirriemuir, St Andrews, Crieff, Comrie, Perth. We had regular days for going to Kirriemuir or Brechin or Comrie and all those other places, and for selling the onions in streets in Dundee. We went to a different place every day. When my father got a van we put the bicycles in the van and cycled out from the van with loads of onions once we got to wherever we were going to sell them.

At Crieff there was a big hotel – the Crieff Hydro – with 193 rooms which bought our onions. There was a *cuisto* there, a cook or chef, who bought onions from my father. He bought a lot of onions – sixty bunches! Oh, it was a very big hotel. We went to the Crieff Hydro every three weeks and they always bought onions from my father. We went to maybe five or six hotels in Crieff to sell the onions but the Hydro was the big one. It bought more onions from my father than anywhere else.

We sold onions to restaurants also, as well as to people at home, and sometimes to schools, too. Schools didn't buy many onions from us, some did but certainly not all of them.

After I'd been working at Dundee as an Onion Johnny for two or three years we moved our place from Dock Street to Rose Lane, which wasn't near the harbour. It was a big house there with three storeys. We moved from Dock Street because the shop there was too small for us. That's why after I'd been there three years or so we decided to go to Rose Lane. Oh, we were glad to move to Rose Lane!

At Rose Lane there weren't any onions stored in the rooms where we slept. The onions were kept in another room. The rooms didn't have walls exactly but planks or boards separating them. I didn't have a room to myself, I shared one with my father. The other Onion Johnnies slept in other rooms. We all had a bed each. None of us slept at Rose Lane beside the onions.

The onions were brought to us in Dundee by a boat that came with them from Roscoff. My father never sailed on the boat with the onions. When we worked in Dock Street, that, of course, was very near the harbour. There were usually two loads of onions that arrived for us at Dundee harbour every onion-selling season. One came on the boat in August, and the other one either in September or October. As soon as the onions were unloaded from the boat I and the other Onion Johnnies carried the onions to the shop. That was part of our work. My father always arranged for, oh, plenty onions to be brought to Dundee.

I worked as a Johnny selling the onions from Monday to Saturday but never on Sunday. We never touched the onions on Sunday, we never sold them that day. On weekdays we started work early, very early, in the morning, oh, at seven o'clock. We worked until lunchtime, about midday, and then we stopped for an hour or so for something to eat. We didn't stop at midday for two hours as in France! One hour was enough. And then we worked on until, oh, about five o'clock. Sometimes we finished a bit earlier than five o'clock, it just depended. But normally it was about five o'clock. At Dundee and all those other places like Perth and Forfar and Crieff we had our customers who bought the onions, and they sold well. So if we were away from Dundee, say, at Perth or Brechin or Crieff, we might finish a bit later than five o'clock, maybe about six or so.

Wherever we were working during the day, we went back to the shop in Dock Street or Rose Lane after we finished. Then after dinner we carried on working there, stringing the onions. Everybody worked at that. We were always working. It was work, work, work all the time. We didn't sit and read in the evening or listen to the radio or watch television. Oh, all the time you worked – except for Sunday. We never worked on Sunday, well, we never sold onions on Sunday. But we worked at stringing them on Sunday. We were in the shop then. We didn't stop working. It was non-stop! We never had holidays, we never had a day off.

On Sundays I never went to church in Dundee. Oh, there were plenty of churches in Dundee – Catholic and Protestant. But I never went to church there. Normally I went to church when I was at home in Roscoff. We were Catholics. My parents and I went every Sunday when my father and I were at home. But not in Dundee. I didn't go there because, well, they didn't use the same language. I had difficulty in following the mass. They weren't the same as in Brittany. So I said, 'No, I don't go to church.' And I never went there.

As I say, we didn't watch TV or listen to the radio. We had a radio at home at Roscoff but I don't think we had a radio at the shop the first year or so I was at Dundee. And I wasn't a reader. I didn't read newspapers, the Scottish or English newspapers. We had no time to look at the papers. Our time in the shop was spent stringing the onions! The Johnnies didn't have leisure really, it was all work.

You went to the cemetery at *Toussaint*, All Saints' Day, the 1st of November. That's what was done at home at Roscoff, too. On the 1st of November you didn't work at all. You went to church. You always went that day to the cemetery. And you went to the cemetery that day as a mark of respect for the dead. There was always great respect for the dead shown that day, *Toussaint*. That was always the case. At home in the afternoon all the young people like us played pontoon. So as Onion Johnnies we did that at Dundee, too, and then when the pubs opened we had a drink there after six o'clock. That was all we did on the 1st of November.

I remember there was an Onion Johnny buried in Lochee cemetery at Dundee. His name was Appamont. He was sailing on a boat loaded with onions that was going to Scotland. Then I don't know quite what happened. He apparently slipped on board the boat and fell and struck his head. He died afterward and he was buried at Lochee.

I never felt homesick at Dundee. I wrote home to my mother every week, and my mother sent a letter to me and my father every week.

The customers I sold the onions to in Scotland were polite and friendly. Oh, occasionally when I rang a customer's bell, you know: 'Oh, go away. I'm no' . . . We have plenty onions here. We dinnae want any onions.' I remember once there was a big man who seemed to be hopping mad because I had rung his bell. 'Excuse me,' I said, 'but I'm being polite to you.' I don't know what he was going to do to me, maybe give me a kick on the backside, I don't know. But there weren't many people like that. Most people were friendly and polite.

I made some friends among the Scots people at Dundee. There was an old couple called Mr and Mrs William Dick. They lived at No. 8 Jura Street in Dundee. Madame Dick had been a nurse during the First World War. She nursed the men wounded at the front. That was how Mr Dick had met her. They got married and came to live at Dundee. They were in a flat on the second floor at No. 8 Jura Street. When I rang their bell to sell the onions they would say, 'You want a cup o' tea?' 'Yes, yes,' I said, 'I'd like a cup o' tea.' My father and his brother, my uncle, they went also to Mr and Mrs Dick's sometimes. They were good friends. But by the time my father left Dundee Mr and Mrs Dick were no longer in good health. They were already ill then. Mr Dick had asked to be buried when he died in Lochee cemetery beside Appamont, the Onion Johnny who died as a result of the accident on the boat and was buried there. Mr Dick had said to my father, 'If I'm going to die I want to be buried beside the Frenchman, beside Appamont.'

Some other customers, too, but not a lot of them, said to me, 'Oh, come in and have a cup o' tea.' I got a biscuit or sometimes cake.

I remember there was also a Protestant pastor, a kind of chief, Monsieur Bell, Reverend Bell. He was in charge of a whole area. He bought onions from us, too. He spoke French very well. He and his wife came to see my father at Roscoff. They had visited everything at Roscoff. They were at the church there, everything. They had visited all the places around. Rev. Bell had written a book. I still have a copy of it.

The onions we sold in Dundee were grown on my father's farm at Roscoff. They were just called *oignons rosés de Roscoff* - pink Roscoff onions. Oh, they were very good onions. Some of the onions I see being sold now are not so good as they were. Now some of them are very hard to eat – they'd break your teeth! But our pink Roscoff onions have got a good smell and it's very easy to eat them. Onions from Brittany really were good quality. It was the land, the soil, the onions tasted good. It's really good soil at Roscoff for growing onions. It's not the same soil in England, it's a different soil there. At Dundee some people grew onions in their gardens. Some of them said to me, 'Oh, we have onions in our garden – plenty in our garden.' But the pink onions from Roscoff were really good quality. Of course, we also had yellow onions and red onions, but the pink ones were best.

There was yellow in Spanish onions, too. But there were never any Spanish men in Dundee selling their onions. There were Spanish onions there but no Spanish men selling them!

In earlier times there were quite a number of Breton Onion Johnnies at Dundee. But when I was there, there was just my father's company of six or seven of us and there was one other man. He said, 'I go to every street in Dundee.' Before and after the 1939–45 War there were some Onion Johnnies based at Perth. There were two or three of them there when I was first at Dundee. There was Jean-Marie Roignant and Louis Poisson. But they're dead now. Then Isidore Chapalain and one or two others went to sell onions in Aberdeen. But they're dead now, too.

In earlier days there were about 200 or 300 Onion Johnnies who went to England and Scotland to sell the onions. I've heard my father say that there some Johnnies who went from Roscoff to sell onions in Ireland, too – Northern Ireland, I think. But there their bunches of onions were stolen from them. After that, I think, the Johnnies stopped going to Ireland and they went only to England, Scotland, and Wales. I don't know but I think it was because the Johnnies were Bretons and Catholics that they had difficulties in Northern Ireland. So only one or two Johnnies tried to sell onions there but they didn't succeed. I've heard it said they were very funny people in Northern Ireland, they didn't like to buy onions from Brittany, and that they were all robbers! But that's just what I heard.

When I used to ring a customer's bell at Dundee and said to

her, 'You want some onions, Missus, please?' She says, 'How much?' '3s.9d.' That was the price then, 3s.9d. a bunch. She would say, 'Oh, well, yes, yes, that's good.' But other people would say, 'Oh, I go to the shop if I want onions. I go to the shop at the corner to get them.' In a bunch there were about four pounds of onions, so the price then was about a shilling a pound. That was dearer than people would buy them for in the shops. In a shop you got onions then for 6d. a pound. The Breton onions were dearer but were good quality. The shop onions were not so good.

Every Onion Johnny was paid according to the work he did. We were paid at the end of the onion-selling season. During the season my father would give me some coppers to go to the cinema with – some pocket money like that. I didn't smoke, so I didn't need money for cigarettes. My father bought the food and drink we ate at the shop. We ate as at home – meat, bread, and so on. If we hadn't eaten, well, we wouldn't have been able to stand up and do our work! But we got paid at the end of the season, not before. So I worked for my father for six months, from July to Christmas and then my father paid me for my work. It was a round sum I was paid. I don't remember now how much I was paid for it's a long time ago. But I never felt I was a rich man! No, I was a very poor man! For the money we had to work every day – no work, no money.

There was never a trade union or *syndicat* among the Onion Johnnies at Dundee, there was nothing like that. There were a lot of unions in France but there was never one for Johnnies at Dundee.

Well, I was an Onion Johnny at Dundee for about a dozen years, from 1951 to about 1963 or 1964. It was then I stopped selling onions in Dundee. By that time my father was getting old. We still had the small farm at Roscoff and my mother couldn't manage it by herself. So I decided I had better stay at home at Roscoff and work on the farm to help my mother and father.

Jean-Marie Tanguy

Looking back on those years I worked as a Johnny at Dundee, it was very hard work. For a young fellow like me it was very hard. But all of us Johnnies there got on well together. There were no quarrels among us and we were all friendly with each other. The people, our customers, were friendly, never unfriendly or hostile. I never felt I wanted to do any other kind of job at home in Brittany or at Dundee. You left home to sell the onions and then you came to like the job. Oh, we liked our *métier*, our job of selling the onions. Well, we had to work, didn't we, to earn our crust of bread? We wouldn't have been able to do that if we'd just stayed at home in Roscoff.

GUY LE BIHAN

My wife and I were married on the 3rd of July 1957 and I went away on the 25th of July to Scotland for the first time to start work as an Onion Johnny at Ayr. My father-in-law was already an Onion Johnny there and it was his idea that I should go and work with him.

I was born on the 15th of December 1930 in Brittany at Santec, just 300 metres away from where I live now. I've no' moved very far!

My father was a farmer who owned his own farm. It was quite a small farm, only four or five hectares – about 10 or 12 acres. My father was never an Onion Johnny – unlike my father-in-law and his father and other members of his family. My father was born in 1896, so he was 43 when the 1939–45 War began, and as he had three children he wasn't called up to the French forces.

My mother had worked in the fields before she was married. She was an orphan, because her father had been killed in the First World War, in 1914. Her mother, my grandmother, had a difficult time because she was left then to bring up a family of four children. The youngest child was born in 1914 and my grandfather was killed soon after that. My mother never really knew her father, she was too young to remember him.

War played a big part in the lives of our families, because my father-in-law, with whom I went to work at Ayr, was a prisoner-of-war in Germany for five years during the Second World War. And so were both his brothers.

I began school at Santec when I was five, in 1935. That first school was for boys and girls. Then after a year there I went to a school for boys and I remained at that school until I left when I was 14. I liked the school. There were some subjects that interested me more than others but I suppose I was just an average pupil. But things were very difficult, you know, because after I'd been three years or so at the school the war broke out and there was the German occupation of France from 1940 until 1944. We couldn't go to the school at St Pol de Léon, about four kilometres away from Santec, because there was no transport to take us there and back. And there were no men teachers, only women, because of the war.

During the occupation the Germans were everywhere on the coast of Brittany. Finistère, our *département* or region, was a very strategic area. So there were a lot of German soldiers at Roscoff, four kilometres from Santec, and along the coast. That made things very difficult for all the people round about Santec, Roscoff and St Pol de Léon. The school was open every day the usual hours and I went every day, but you were always aware as a boy of the German occupation around you. Of course, after the war you realised that some of our local people had been in the Resistance against the Germans.

My family – I had a brother and a sister – were more fortunate than some other people living in the towns, because we had my father's small farm (I was going to say wee farm, as you say in Scotland.) We had three cows, so we had milk and butter. We kept a pig to kill, so we also got bacon and pork and ham. We kept hens, too, so we had eggs. And we grew vegetables, so we had plenty of onions and potatoes. We always had some food. But nonetheless things were very difficult.

In 1944, after the D-Day landings in Normandy in June, the Liberation from the Germans took place at St Pol de Léon in August. Somebody said the Americans had reached Morlaix, about 25 kilometres east of Santec. So there was fighting at St Pol de Léon on the 6th of August between the Resistance and the Germans. I think about 25 were killed in the fighting just near the cathedral. It was very, very sad.

It was just at that time, in the summer of 1944, I left school. As a boy I didn't have any particular ambitions. I always believed that I would work like my father on the land, on our farm. So that's what I did when I left school, helping my father on the farm. I had to do every kind of job in the fields.

Well, I worked on the farm for about twelve or thirteen years, until I was 27. I was married, as I've said, at the beginning of July 1957. It was only then that I went for the first time to Scotland as an Onion Johnny. It was my father-in-law's idea, he encouraged me to do that. He had first gone to Britain to sell onions after the 1939–45 War. He was near London at first, at Reading, then he went to Hounslow. Then he went up to Scotland with his brother-in-law, who'd been working at Ayr as an Onion Johnny even before the war.

When I arrived with my father-in-law at Ayr in July 1957 I found we were based at a stables there. We had thirty tons of onions to sell, so we needed a lot of space. So we put the onions in the stables, which were in the centre of Ayr. But we didn't live ourselves in the stables, we lived in a house near the stables. It was quite a comfortable house. It had four rooms. Living conditions there were good. There was running water in the house and a bath, a flush toilet, and electric light.

Later on we moved to live at a farm. The town of Ayr had bought this farm to build houses on. So we had the house and also accommodation for the onions. That was quite a comfortable place, too.

In both places we had more or less a room each to live in and sleep in. There were five of us. There was my father-in-law and myself, and his brother-in-law and his son. And there was a Johnny to do the stringing of the onions.

At that time at Ayr there was also another company of

Onion Johnnies – a man and his two boys. They were quite separate from our company. So when I first went to Ayr in 1957 there were eight Onion Johnnies in the town, five in our company and three in the other one.

When I first began as a Johnny I didn't speak any English at all. But, you know, to sell onions you don't need to speak. All you needed to know was the price of the onions and how many – *combien* - the customer wanted. At first I got the same kind of answers when I rang the door bells: 'Oh, we have enough.' 'We have plenty of onions in the garden.' 'When will you be back again?' So after I had been working for a week or two these became familiar words to me. And from then *voilà* I began to be able to understand and speak English.

In the morning I got up at six o'clock and then got washed and had some breakfast and I was ready to go out selling the onions usually from about 8 or 8.30 a.m. There wasn't any point in going earlier because some of the customers wouldn't be up out of their beds before then. But of course the time you started depended, too, on the area you were going to to sell the onions.

Usually I had a sandwich between half-past eleven and twelve midday, because that was a quiet time. Then at lunch time, say from midday, some people came home and so we had to get these people in between twelve midday and about two o'clock in the afternoon. After that, around three and four o'clock, it was again very quiet for us because people went shopping. Then at five or six o'clock they came back home again. So there were certain times of the day when you could expect to sell more onions than at other times. The best times were early morning, lunchtime or after five o'clock.

You came to know your regular customers. Some were schoolteachers so they had to be at their school for nine o'clock in the morning. So you had to go and see them earlier in the morning or maybe at lunchtime when they came home again, or after five o'clock. I found lunchtime was a very good time for selling the onions and then teatime again. But after 2.30 p.m. or 3 p.m. it was very difficult. Even the older women at home had a sleep then! So they wouldn't be pleased if they heard me ringing their bell, *bbbrrrrrhhh*! Oh, you had to be diplomatic.

Of course, as the years passed social conditions were changing. More women were going out to work during the day, whereas in earlier years women had generally remained at home and worked in the house and not so many had jobs outside it. It made life more difficult for us as Onion Johnnies if there wasn't a woman at home to buy our onions.

I don't think we had to be specially careful about ringing the bell *bbbrrrrrhhh* if there was maybe a miner in the house who was sleeping after working night shift. In miners' houses the wife was usually at home to answer the door.

We didn't return at lunchtime to the stables, or later the farm, where we were based in Ayr. As I say, I usually had a sandwich about half-past eleven. And then, well, about three or four o'clock in the afternoon we had time to go in and get a cup of tea in a cafe. I didn't carry a thermos flask or a tea bottle. So I went into a cafe. I usually went to the same cafe in Ayr. It was an Italian cafe and they bought our onions, too. Italian people like onions and garlic. They bought ours, so I bought their tea. It was usually tea I used to drink there. I liked tea and it was better in Scotland than in Brittany. I think it's different water. I don't know, but tea is very good in Scotland. And going into the Italian cafe in Ayr maybe helped our business as well, *voilà*. The more cups of tea I bought there, perhaps the more they bought our onions and garlic.

Well, in the afternoons and evenings we worked on until maybe five or six or sometimes seven o'clock. But we never came home with a string of onions. All of them had to be sold. So some days the time when we finished selling them varied. But it wasn't often later than about seven o'clock. If you rang the bell at seven o'clock people said, 'I knew who it was, I knew it was you.' They were expecting the Onion Johnny. In the morning it was the same. It was the same people you went to early in the morning so they didn't worry when you rang the bell. Punctuality was important. But we always tried never to go back home to the stables or the farm with our onions unsold – except if you had broken down with the van or something like that. But normally the onions had to be sold. That wasn't because we were afraid the onions would go soft. It was because, well, you went here or there and you knew how many strings of onions you could expect to sell. If you ended up, maybe in Kilmarnock, with maybe thirty onions still unsold, well, you would have to try to sell them to other people than your regular customers. It was a matter of pride almost for the Onion Johnnies not to return with unsold onions!

When we finished work in the evening, whether it was five or six or seven o'clock, we went back home to the stables or the farm and had our dinner then. After that we worked at stringing the onions until bedtime. Bedtime was sometimes about eleven.

On Saturdays we worked, too, at selling the onions but we usually finished earlier on Saturday, maybe at three o'clock or half-past three. Then on Sundays sometimes four of us – my father-in-law, his brother-in-law and his son, and me – went to cut rushes in the fields, for stringing the onions. We had the permission of the farmer to cut the rushes – well, we gave him a few onions in payment for them. The rushes were strong and they were better than using straw or hay for the stringing. It was easier, too, to use rushes. There were plenty of rushes so that's what we used at Ayr.

Beginning the selling of the onions was really hard when I first went to Ayr in 1957. At that time, when there were a lot of Johnnies there, you could find some other Johnny had been there at the customer's door one or two days before you. There was competition. The Johnnies then didn't organise the work so that you didn't go to a door that somebody else had been to two or three days before. Oh, there was competition between the different companies of Johnnies! As well as the eight Johnnies in the two companies at Ayr, there were maybe at that time at Glasgow twenty Johnnies, oh, maybe more. And the Glasgow Johnnies came down to Ayrshire to sell their onions as well.

There was one Johnny – Pencolo: in Breton that meant *Tête de Paille*, Strawhead. Oh, he was well known. He came from Roscoff. He went after the 1939–45 War to work in Glasgow as a Johnny. Before the war he had worked down in England somewhere, Plymouth or somewhere. He was working just on his own, not in a company of Johnnies. So he had to go to every house to make his living. And if you sold onions to a house that he thought was his customer, oh! 'That is my customer. You're no' allowed to come here.' He was very bad. But he managed to make a living eventually.

It wasn't common for Onion Johnnies to work on their own. It wasn't easy to make a living out of selling the onions if you were on your own. Once you finished work selling them, you had to come home and make the strings yourself. You didn't have a division of labour, where one Johnny or more sold the onions, and another or others were stringing them in the shop. You really had to have a worker, *un ouvrier*, who strung the onions all day long, preparing them for the sellers to go out the next day and sell them. If I'd been on my own at Ayr as Pencolo was in Glasgow I'd have had to spend hours every day stringing the onions and then I wouldn't have had so long to sell them. So it would have been very difficult.

I remember there was another Onion Johnny who worked on his own at Carlisle. He was called Per-a-Peskic. He was on his own there. He didn't have his wife or anybody else with him. He was stringing the onions and selling them himself. There was no other Johnny with him. So it must have been difficult for him.

That was why Onion Johnnies usually worked in groups, in companies, of maybe four or five or eight or nine, and so on. Of course, if there were too many Johnnies in a company it was no' easy either. The ideal number was maybe three or four. So there was competition then. You couldn't work on your own very easily and make a success of it.

It wasn't only in Ayr that we sold the onions. We sold them up along the coast of Ayrshire at Irvine, Saltcoats, West Kilbride, and into Largs. And then inland to Kilbirnie, Beith, Kilwinning, Kilmarnock, and even as far as at Newton Mearns in Renfrewshire, then down to Mauchline, Cumnock, New Cumnock, and Dalmellington. We went up the Irvine Valley to Newmilns and Darvel, and down the Ayrshire coast from Ayr to Girvan and then on to Stranraer. It was a big area.

When we were selling the onions in Ayr or just around Ayr we just went with the onions loaded on our bikes. But when we went to those other places like Stranraer or Kilmarnock or Largs or Darvel that were far away from Ayr we went in a van. We filled the van with onions and put the bikes into it, too. We used the van as a base, a kind of depot. When we arrived wherever we were going for that day we went out on our own with our bikes with the onions and then when we had sold them we came back to the van for more. That was the usual arrangement. We didn't use the van when we were selling the onions in Ayr itself, just the bikes.

At first it was an Austin van. It was quite a big van. It could hold the four of us and our bikes and a whole lot of onions. Later on we had a Bedford van. It was quite big, too. It was easy because it had a sliding door. And when the weather was nice you didn't need to shut the sliding door. You could drive along on a sunny warm day with the sliding door open. It helped to advertise our onions and garlic if the door was open because of the good smell that came from them!

Onion Johnnies

Wherever we went outside Ayr with the van we always returned home to the stables or farm that evening. We came back every day. We never slept overnight in the van. I've heard that some Onion Johnnies in the north of Scotland – Henri Chapalain was one – would go away from Aberdeen for a week to sell the onions and they would sleep in the van because the distances they had to travel to sell their onions were so great. But we never did that in Ayrshire.

We had a kind of cycle of visits. Kilmarnock was every week on a Friday. We went every week there because Friday was the pay day in Kilmarnock. There was a lot of work in Kilmarnock at that time. So on Friday night there was plenty of money! It was sensible for us to sell the onions to people who had money to pay for them. Every fourth Saturday we went to Stranraer. And then on another Saturday during the month we went to Kilbirne, Beith and some other places in north Ayrshire. And on a third Saturday we went up the Irvine Valley to Newmilns and Darvel. And I think the other Saturday we went to Kilwinning and Irvine.

Newmilns and Darvel were textile towns then and I think the wages were not very good. That was why we went on a Saturday, pay day. And then there were a lot of miners in towns like Cumnock and New Cumnock and Dalmellington, and it was very hard there. Dalmellington was away over the moors, an isolated place. The miners, when they had money, bought more onions from us than teachers did. I think the miners were eating the onions with mince and steak. When customers were eating mince and steak they were more likely to buy our onions than when they were eating maybe fish.

In a string or *ficelle* of onions there might be five, six or seven onions, somewhere about that number. The weight of a string or *ficelle* would be about one and a half kilos, or three and a half pounds. There were two strings in a bunch or *botte* of onions. So in a bunch or *botte* there'd be twice as many onions, around a dozen. The weight of a bunch or *botte* would be about three kilos – about seven pounds. When I set off in the morning on my bike at Ayr I'd have maybe thirty bunches hanging from the handlebars or over the carrier above the back wheel. So that would be about 350 or 360 onions altogether. Oh, it was very heavy!

Later on at Ayr when I was just myself I sold sometimes 140 or 160 bunches of onions like that every day. That would be almost 2,000 onions a day. I'm not telling fibs! In fact, I kept a note, a diary, at the time of where I went to sell the onions and how many bunches I sold. It says: 'Kilmarnock – 152. Beith – 160 by 5.15 p.m. Newton Mearns: 152 by 7.15 p.m.' So it's not a joke! It's really true.[26]

I liked Ayr. It was an attractive town. I liked the people at Ayr. I found they were very, very friendly. The town had associations with Robert Burns. I was interested in Burns. I read some of his poems and still have a copy of a book of his poems. I liked to listen, too, to his songs.

But people in Ayrshire were generally very, very friendly. You were politely received, even if they didn't always buy the onions. Very often they told you, 'Come in. Have a cup o' tea.' It was usually tea or coffee they offered you – at Christmas and New Year, whisky. Scotland is different from England and after New Year in Scotland you got 'your New Year'. But even after it I kept to the left side of the road! You came to know every family. One customer I had they had a little girl who was only two years old. Well, many years later my wife and I were invited to her wedding in Scotland. It was the first time my wife had been to Scotland.

Sometimes you found customers who were anxious to speak to you in French – schoolteachers, or students maybe or other young ones of families. They sort of practised their French on you. Then there were two or three customers who were French themselves. I remember two ladies who came from Dieppe and from Calais. They had married Scotsmen after the 1939–45 War. It was nice to be able to speak in French with them.

I never did get away from Ayr for a holiday anywhere else in Scotland, like the Highlands. You would never have time for a holiday. Well, in Ayr anyway we were at the seaside. But I never had a holiday of any kind while I worked as an Onion Johnny in Scotland.

Every year for over twenty years I went there for the onion-selling season, from the end of July or the beginning of August until Christmas or New Year. Sometimes I was back home at Santec for Christmas, but not always. You know, from about 1971 there was a ferry from Roscoff and we loaded a lorry with onions to cross on the ferry. When the onions were all sold, then we came back home. By about that time I was at Ayr just myself and it was too much to have two lorries with onions. So when the one lorry load was sold – that was it, finish: I came back home. In earlier years loads of onions went three times in the season to Leith: one in August, the second one at the end of September, and the third one at the beginning of December, because in those days some of the Johnnies stayed on working in Scotland until March. They were sent down then from Leith to us at Ayr. So at that time you could get more onions if you wanted them, there was always a supply coming in. But later on, as I say, that wasn't so any longer and it made things more difficult.

Every year, too, when I went back home at the end of the season to Santec I worked on my father-in-law's small farm there. Then in the next July or August I went back again to Ayr. So it was six months at home in Santec with my wife and family, then six months working as a Johnny again at Ayr. It wasn't easy for my wife when I was away in Scotland. As I've said, I first went away to become an Onion Johnny in 1957 just three weeks after we were married. We were young. There wasn't any telephone we could use in those days. And as the years passed we had three children. It was my wife really who had to see to their schooling and all that. She also had to attend to the business of buying and sending loads of onions to us in Ayr. That was a lot of work for her. And she had to look after my father-in-law's small farm, too, when he and I were away. She had her mother at Santec, but otherwise my wife was on her own for six months every year. Oh, it was difficult for her. I wrote home to my wife two or three times a week from Ayr, and she wrote to me that often, too.

Writing home took up some of the little free time I had after a day's work selling the onions and then helping to string them once we were back to the stables or farm at Ayr in the evening. As I say, you never really got spare time as an Onion Johnny. I went swimming sometimes because there was a pool near us in Ayr. But I never played golf or went to watch football matches there. I wasn't interested much in football, not even at Santec. And I certainly didn't go out cycling for recreation! On a Saturday I went out to the pub – the Castle Bar, near the harbour in Ayr – with Pierre Tanguy, the Johnny who was stringing the onions for us. Pierre Tanguy never went out anywhere during the week but just strung the onions all the time for us in the stables or later at the farm. So on Saturday night we went out to the pub with him. The owner of the pub was very nice, and we went there for an hour or so on a Saturday night and had a glass of beer, and then we went back home again.

On Sunday I went to mass. I was a regular attender and went every Sunday. Then, as I've said, on Sunday afternoons we went and cut rushes in the fields for stringing the onions.

Well, I was an Onion Johnny at Ayr for twenty years, from 1957 until 1978. Soon after I went there, oh, from about the 1960s, the number of Onion Johnnies was declining. After about 1966 I was at Ayr just by myself, with Pierre Tanguy who strung the onions. Pierre didn't sell the onions, he only strung them. A bit later on my two sons, who were at school, then at college, came to help us just for the summer holidays. The decline in the number of Johnnies made it easier for us. Well, when you went to Kilmarnock or to Stranraer and so on, there was now nobody else, no other Johnnies had been there just before you. We didn't have competitors as we had had before.

By that time the older Onion Johnnies like my father-in-law and Jean Saout and some others had retired or were retiring. And Johnnies' sons, you know, didn't bother about taking up the job, because, well, it was a hard life. It had been a hard life for me and the others. But, you know, I liked it. I liked the people. It wasn't that there was more employment around Roscoff and Santec and St Pol de Léon by the time sons were growing up so that they didn't need to become Onion Johnnies. It wasn't that. But there was a big change for young people at home in Brittany and everywhere. There was a new generation. I don't think it was that young people were lazy. It was a difference in the generations. Well, the young people remained at school or college until they were 20 or more. I and other Onion Johnnies had left school when we were fourteen or younger. So after the young people left school or college they got a job of some kind at home in Brittany. My wife and I, for instance, have two sons and a daughter. The girl's teaching now in St Malo. Her husband is in electronics. Our oldest son is manager in the Crédit Agricole bank in Paimpol, and our other boy is an engineer in Rennes. So they certainly wouldn't be interested in giving up those jobs and going to sell onions in Scotland! Young people have a higher level of education than we and the older Johnnies – Ingan Johnnies, as we were called in Scotland – ever had and there was more variety of employment for them than there was for us, their parents or grandparents. It wasn't because they were lazy they didn't become Onion Johnnies, because they have had to work hard to become teachers and managers and engineers and so on. But it was a different world for them from what it was for us older ones. So I think that was the main reason for the decline in the number of Onion Johnnies in Ayrshire, in Scotland, and in Britain as a whole.

In my own case, as I say, I remained an Onion Johnny at Ayr until 1978. My father-in-law, who was born in 1911, had retired from selling the onions about 1966. So from 1978 I had to stay at home in Santec. By then my father-in-law was 69. He and my wife were looking after the farm. He was just feeling too old for it, it was too much for him. So I had to stop work as a Johnny at Ayr and go home and work the farm at Santec.

I was very, very sad at having to give up being an Onion Johnny. And, you know, when you saw the remaining Johnnies going away in July or August to work on the other side of the English Channel it was very sad. It was a way of life I'd had for twenty years. When I came back home at first I missed working with my customers at Ayr and in Ayrshire. I found it difficult to come to terms with. As a Johnny I was moving around selling the onions all the time. One day you were in Ayr, another at Kilmarnock, another at Largs or Stranraer, and so on. Then I was back home working on my father-in-law's farm, quite a small farm – and you're not moving away every day, you know, as you did selling the onions. Oh, it was difficult to get used to at first. I missed the contact, too, with my customers.

Well, it's very sad to think now about the disappearance of the Onion Johnnies from Scotland. There's nobody else going back there. We worked hard to build the businesses there up, to find the customers. I don't know where people in Scotland are buying their onions now. Is it from the supermarkets? But that's no' as good, no' as good, because the pink onions of Santec and Roscoff and St Pol de Léon were very good onions.

YVES ROLLAND

I was born, the youngest of three brothers and three sisters, at St Pol de Léon in Brittany at the end of the Second World War, on 29 May 1945. Marie, my oldest sister, was twenty years older than me, then after her came Hélène and Françoise, then my two brothers Pierre and Jean. Pierre was about two years older than Jean, and between Jean and me I think there were another two-and-a-half years. Marie was already a young woman by the time I was born, and while I was growing up she was married and away from our home.

My father was a farm worker all his working life, never an Onion Johnny. He worked on farms that grew all sorts of vegetables, as most of the farms around St Pol did. Some of the farms grew grain but very, very few. More or less it was all vegetables – cauliflowers were the main crop at that time, and there were artichokes, onions, potatoes, and carrots. There were cabbages as well but not really many. You've got to go up to the Côtes du Nord further east in Brittany to get the cabbages. It was early season vegetables my father worked with on the farms most of the time. He did that all his life, from leaving school until he retired.

My father was born in 1902 so he was too young to fight in the 1914–18 War. He didnae go to the Second World War either – and I think in that case that was because of the family. I think he was excused military service because of the number of kids he had. He had to stay at home for the sake of the kids, or something like that. I think there was some government regulation that if a father had more than two or three children he wasn't called up to the Forces. At any rate he didn't fight in either of the two wars.

My dad had a hard life. I can't remember exactly the age he was when he left school but it was ten or twelve, I think. As soon as you were big enough in those days you had to start to work. Most of what they learned was just through life, you know, just from practical experience. My father was a good worker. He used to start work at daybreak and finish when the light was off. Oh, long hours, and six days a week – Monday to Saturday. He didn't work on Sunday: Sunday normally was for going to mass. And he never had holidays in the summer, not even a day off occasionally. Every day in his life he was working, except on Sundays and the 14th of July – Bastille Day: it's a national holiday.

After the Second World War, when I was young, my dad used to go to work at the sugar beet near Paris for maybe two months at a time. He used to do that as well, because he was earning good money at it. Well, my dad was 81 when he died, so that was about 1983.

My mum was born in Cléder, a village about eight miles from Roscoff. She told me she never went to school, more or less like, you know. At that time there was no law for that kind of thing. As soon as you were big enough you had to work. My mum and my dad were both able to read and write. They must have been to school but it's difficult to know what they did there. As I say, my dad stayed at school, I think, until he was twelve and my mum until she was ten or something. My mum didnae stay at school as long as my dad, that I know.

Before she got married, it was a hell of a life for my mum as well because she used to work for a bakery. She used to deliver the bread, and believe it or not she used to go delivering, I would say, thirty kilometres around. She delivered the bread with a horse and cart – we called the cart a *charrette*, a two-wheeled trap. That's what she used to do when she was young. So a hell of a life as well! I would reckon she had started at the bakery when she left school but I don't know for sure because, as I say, I never asked questions. But that's the only thing, the only job she did I heard about. She stopped working at the bakery when she got married. At that time when a girl got married she didn't normally carry on working outside the house, because, I mean, you're there normally to provide for your family. And of course in time my mum had six children, as I say.

I don't know what my grandfather – my mother's father – did for a living. I don't know if he was in the bakery, too. I cannae say, I'm no' sure. I can't remember seeing my grandparents on my mother's side. They had maybe passed away by the time I was growing up and I have no recollection of them.

I never saw my other grandfather either, my father's father. I don't know if he died before I was born because I never enquired. You know, when you're young you don't enquire about those sort of things. You don't even think about it. But I've heard more or less he was a clog maker. My father said my grandfather used to do that. He was working for himself. He didn't employ any workers, no' that I know of anyway. My dad would have told me that if he had. I've heard he was doing it from door to door. At that time it was really quite a skilled job, being a clog maker. It was all done by hand an' a'. You don't see those sort of clogs any more nowadays. At that time, you see, they had only wood inside. I remember when I was very young my dad wore clogs but no socks – jist bare feet. But they used to wear straw in them. They used to cut the straw and put it into the clogs. Actually it was warm. That's what my dad used to wear when I was young but I never did. I always had shoes or boots.

I can't go back in the family beyond my grandparents. Oh, I never heard what my great-grandfathers did! But so far as I know the family had always lived at St Pol de Léon or around there.

At home when I was young my mum and dad spoke Breton but normally they spoke just French. Well, but there's only a few words of Breton that I know. My oldest brother Pierre he spoke Breton better than my mum and dad. He always lived near home somewhere so he would be more in the daily habit of speaking Breton. He never came to Scotland or England to work as an Onion Johnny.

I was born at St Pol de Léon as I've said, but actually we lived out in the countryside, two or three kilometres from St Pol. My mum and dad lived in a house out in the country that had a piece of ground where we could raise rabbits, chickens and goats. Some things I can't remember but we had, I think, one or two cows and lambs and pigs. We did have pigs because they used to kill them. So while my dad was working for a wage as a day labourer on farms we also as a family had those animals. You needed to have them, because otherwise at that time you couldn't live with a family to keep. The wages were too small. So the cows and maybe the goats gave us milk and the pigs gave us meat, and on the piece of ground we could grow our own vegetables.

So I grew up in that house about three kilometres from St Pol. I lived there with my family till I was about six or seven years old. I don't really know how many rooms that house had – it must have been, I would say, four bedrooms. It was quite a sizeable house. We used to share rooms at that time. I think the three of us boys were in the same room. And if my recollection is right we used to have at that time the sort of bunk bed that people have now. Yet it was totally different because we used to have a big straw mattress. The bed was closed like, you know – it was against the wall and it was a big square with a curtain. You went in and the bed was closed off with the curtain.

The girls were in another room. My parents always slept in one of the other rooms, they didn't sleep in the kitchen. I'm no' sure but I think we had electricity in that house. Yet I remember lamps there, too – sort of paraffin lamps. So maybe it was lamps at first and then later electricity. There was no bath or toilet. It was a dry toilet. There was no running water, no tap, in the house. There was a well. It was quite near the house, and they used to drop the bucket into the well and just wind the bucket up with water in it. We used to play with the bucket as children. So getting water was a lot of extra work for my mother in a sense but, I mean, people at that time didn't bother because it wasn't a bother at all. People were born into those conditions. It's the way you're born, the way you're brought up that makes the difference.

When I was about six or seven years old, as I say, we moved to another house that was nearer to St Pol de Léon. It was about 800 metres – half a mile – from the centre of St Pol. It was the farmer who had the farm where my dad used to work who built that house for my dad and our family to come and stay. My dad was very friendly with that farmer because I think he worked with him for more than twenty years. He always worked with that same farmer while I was growing up.

That second house nearer St Pol was about the same size as the first one. But it had electricity: that was a luxury. It was a dry toilet there, too, though. At that time there weren't so many flush toilets. There was no bath or shower in the second house either, but we did have a tap with running water in the house – cold water only. We used to bath ourselves in a tub, a tin bath. It was more or less a case the girls would bath first and the boys would be kept away in the room. Then the girls would go into the room and the boys would be bathed.

I was five or six, I think – it could have been four, mind, I'm no' really sure – when I started school at St Pol de Léon. We used to go to school on foot from that first house in the countryside. That was normal at that time – no school transport in those days! There were two schools in St Pol. There was one for the Catholics and the other was the council or state school. So when we were young we were put in the Catholic school. It was run by the church and actually the Catholic schools they're all right, you know.

I got on very, very well at the school. I was quite good in all subjects. But my best was arithmetic. I still am good at that actually. I still use my head – I don't like very much using gadgets such as calculators. Nowadays at the schools they don't use their brains. The day the machine won't be there the pupils – people – won't be able to do anything. Well, the machine'll master some but no' me, for sure: I hate machines.

As a boy I wasn't much interested in playing football or reading or swimming. We used to play cowboys and Indians more or less. But we were interested in other things, like working. We lived beside the sea, you see. It was no' far, about a mile. So sometimes what we used to do was to go and catch or gather cockles and all sorts of shellfish. And we used to bring them home for tea at night. We didn't try to sell them, it was only for our own eating. We preferred to do that than anything else. We did play football as well but not as an organised team. That didn't exist where I belonged and I don't know if it exists now even. I never played football for the school.

I never had a job like delivering newspapers or milk round the doors while I was at school. You weren't allowed normally to work until you were a certain age. You could only work on a farm. When we had spare time a farmer would ask, 'Could you come and look after the cows? Could you come and do this, could you come and do that?' We didn't use to keep the money for work like that. It was my parents who used to get that money. We would give it to our parents. They kept the money. I didn't get any pocket money. But, I mean, if we needed money we would just go and ask my parents and they would give it to us if they had it to spare.

The only pocket money we had as children was at Christmas time and New Year. At Christmas we used to go to visit our relatives – uncles, aunty, the godfather, and such and such. And everyone you used to go to they used to give you a pound or £2 or £5. And that money was yours. You could do whatever you liked with it.

So as a boy at school I got on very well until I had an accident. I lost an eye. I must have been ten, eleven, twelve at the time. It was an accident with my brother. It was actually my brother who did it. So it took me nearly a year to recover after the accident. I had six or seven operations the same year. I went to hospital, well, a clinic in Morlaix, near St Pol de Léon. So I used to go there. St Pol has no hospital. But I lost the sight of the eye. Well, I felt incapacitated because it doesn't allow me to do the odd thing I would like to do. Even if you'd like to do it you can't do it now, you know.

I don't remember as a boy having any ambitions – nothing like becoming a seaman or a fishermen or driving a railway engine, nothing like that. The only thing that I wanted to do when I was young was to come to Scotland. I don't know what made me think of coming to Scotland. It's very hard to say, because you've got things in your head. You're looking at books, magazines, comics. That's one thing we used to get was comics. And, you know, I was looking at the comics and, oh, some comic would talk about Scotland and all those things they had there. I said, 'I wouldn't mind going there and having a look.'

I was quite happy to leave school. I ken school is good. It's something in itself. But in school you don't learn about living. Most of the things that you learn about life is after you leave school. School gives you an idea, it gives you a wee bit of learning. But the best learning you can have is afterwards. So I've never regretted leaving school when I was 14. My brother Jean was still at school. He had his certificate of studies. I've no certificate. I didn't learn anything as such at school. Well, Jean's not done any better than me actually although he has that certificate. So I left school as soon as I could, as soon as I was 14. I've fought my way all the way from the bottom to the top. I've never had any help from my dad or mum or whatever.

Well, when I left school my dad says to me, 'You've got to find work. There is no other option. You've got to work. You can't stay at home doing nothing. It's either you go to work or you go to college. You'll have to find a job,' he says, 'to sell onions in Scotland.' So I says, 'OK, right.' So I just came to Scotland with a friend of my dad's, a farmer that my dad knew. His name was François Olivier. My dad just said to me there was a friend of a friend who needed somebody to go to Scotland to sell onions with him. And that was it. That's how I came to Scotland. I was only 14½ when I first came here in 1959. By law I wasn't really allowed to work in Scotland at that age. At that time the school leaving age in Scotland was 15. And François, the guy I came with, says to me, 'If you ever get stopped by the police, if they ask what age you are you say 15.' That's what he said to me.

So I set off from home in 1959 when I was 14½ with François Olivier. It wasn't an easy thing to leave home at that age. But at that time you had no option. After I left school that was the first job that came in and that's how it was. My mind wasn't already settled on trying to get to Scotland. It just came like that.

I travelled with François by train from Roscoff to Paris. From Paris we took the train up towards Calais, then Calais-Dover, Dover to London, and London to Edinburgh. It took two nights and one day. It was a very long journey from Roscoff to Edinburgh. Well, afterwards that was the way we always travelled. We used to have sandwiches and everything.

I wish there had been video at that time, because the funniest part about the journey, when all the Onion Johnnies went away to Scotland and England, was that some of the old Ingan Johnnies were badly behaved – well, no' badly behaved but they made you laugh. They used to have wine with them when we left Roscoff and they used to drink themselves nearly to death on the journey. When we arrived at Paris it was a headache. Some of them had to wait so long for the train. So some of them were sprawled about, lying with their arms out at the railway station. Oh, that was a well known fact about some of the old Johnnies. Some of them would hardly behave at all from Roscoff up towards the Channel ferry. After we landed in the south of England, though, when they saw England, they started behaving themselves, because there was no more wine to drink! For me, being young – and I wasn't the only young person travelling to go and sell the onions – it was laughable. We had a good time every time we made the journey. That's why I wish at that time the travelling could have been recorded on video. It would have been really good, like a comic film – *Carry On*, or something like that. It was exactly the same kind of thing – but in the Johnnies' case it was genuine.

That first journey I made from Roscoff to Edinburgh with François Olivier in 1959 was the first time I had been away from home. At home we never went away, we never had a holiday. In fact, I've never had a holiday in my life and my dad and mum never had one either, as I've said. I'd never been further before than to the hospital at Morlaix. I'd never been to Rennes or to Paris or Nantes or anywhere else like that. But though it was my first journey I was no' worried at all. It was either in you go or you don't go, you know.

Well, on that first journey by train from Roscoff I remember there were quite a lot of Onion Johnnies on the train. You see, all the Johnnies tended more or less to set off about the same time to come to England and Scotland. A lot of the Johnnies went to England – to Leeds, Newcastle and the north-east of England, and all those places, and others came to Edinburgh, Glasgow, Aberdeen, Perthshire, and Dundee. So on that first journey I made there would be maybe between fifty and sixty Johnnies on the train. That would be the sort of normal number at that time.

Well, in Leith and Edinburgh alone when I first came in 1959 there used to be about thirty–odd Johnnies. And then there were others based in Glasgow, Dunfermline, Kirkcaldy, Dundee, Perth, Aberdeen, Inverness. I remember there was one Johnny in Dunfermline, and in Perthshire there was another one. And there was a company in Dundee, a company in Aberdeen, and a company in Inverness. These were all French companies. By a company I mean a group of two or three or four Johnnies like. There was no such thing as a formal limited company. It didn't exist. It was just like one boss and three workers, or one boss and one worker or two workers.

So in Inverness, Dunfermline, Dundee at that time there weren't more than two or three or four Johnnies altogether. I think the largest group of Onion Johnnies was then in Leith. You had like Jean Perron there, for instance, and Petit Jean – I can't remember his name now. And in Glasgow there was a group as well but later on they separated, because one was too greedy and the other one, you know, just . . . But at that time, when I first went to Scotland, there could be maybe twelve or fifteen Johnnies working with them. So the system usually was there was one boss, one *patron*, in a group and you could have one, two, three, four, five, maybe up to fifteen Johnnies employed by that one boss. The boss himself came over from Brittany but he was doing the same kind of job as the other Johnnies. He would do the same thing as them but he was at the centre of the whole work. The bosses, the *patrons*, were the people who bought the onions and employed Onion Johnnies like me to sell them. But they sold onions, too, themselves. Well, the bosses' only responsibility was towards the Johnnies, to give them something to eat, somewhere to sleep, and that was it. The rest they looked after themselves. Cooking, for instance – the Johnnies used to cook for themselves. But the boss was at the centre of the work, he paid for the onions and arranged for them to come to Scotland, to Leith or Glasgow or Dundee and so on, wherever his group was based, and he employed the workers, the Johnnies like me.

Some of the Johnnies used to go with the onion boat from Roscoff to Scotland. The boat was loaded in the port in Roscoff and as soon as it was loaded, or the day afterwards, you would leave Roscoff. It took normally about 36 hours to sail from Roscoff to Leith with the onions. When I began as an Onion Johnny in 1959 there was one onion boat which brought the onions for Aberdeen, Dundee, Dunfermline, Perthshire, Leith, and so on. But the onion boat could sometimes come three or four times with more onions during the onion-selling season. In Leith, Saddler's, the shipping company, and another company used to be the companies that had to do with the onion boats.[27] But I know in Roscoff we used to have a company that was called FTO – Fédération du Transport de l'Ouest, or something like that, I think. So those guys would organise the boat at Roscoff and the loading and everything like that. And some of the Onion Johnnies travelled on the onion boat to Scotland. Oh, sometimes it would be a dozen of them, I think. They used to sleep amongst the bloody onions in the hold on the boat! I'm no' joking. Unbelievable, but if you've been brought up that way, well, that's it. Some people would tend to think they were crazy. But that's the way they'd always lived. So for those Johnnies it was the normal way of travelling to Scotland to sell the onions. They certainly didn't travel on the onion boat as passengers in cabins! They just slept in the hold on the cargo of onions. Oh, the captain and the crew were quite willing to let them do that. They used to be quite happy to see them, you know. You can have a good laugh wi' guys like that.

Well, when I came to Leith first when I was 14½ in 1959 François Olivier had his base, his shop, in Admiralty Street. Part of Admiralty Street, not all of it, has been demolished since then. I think you still have Admiralty Street at the top.[28]

Anway at that time I didn't speak the language, I didn't speak English, at all. François used to say to me, 'Don't open the door.' He was afraid, you see, of something happening because I didn't speak English. But the local kids around Admiralty Street they used to come to see me because, I mean, I was a foreigner. They weren't used to seeing a young guy like me. I wasn't shy and I was laughing and things like that with them. But at first I couldn't understand a word they said. I remember one day I said to François, 'That young boy must be in pain. He says, "Aye".' You see, when we say in Breton what sounds like 'aye' it means it hurts.

But it wasn't a big problem for me that at first I knew no English at all, no' really. Two weeks after I came to Leith I was going about on a bicycle with the kids of Admiralty Street and as I didn't know the language I didn't know where we were going. All I knew was that I was going with them on the bike. I got a row from François when I came back. Anyway how I learned English was by talking to people, by reading the paper, by going to the cinema. That's the only way I learned – no school, no nothing. The only books that I had they were the newspapers. One word at a time – I picked up everything. Whatever way you're going to learn the language is no' going to be easy – unless you give yourself to the people. There's lots of people are afraid to make mistakes. But it's no' impolite even if you make a mistake. Actually, it's much easier to learn a language when you're young than when you're old. I never felt shy, right from the beginning with the kids at Admiralty Street I got along fine.

All the Onion Johnnies working in Edinburgh when I first began were based in Leith. They were all around Leith. None of them lived in Edinburgh. In Leith there used to be shops for working in, for storage. And if there was a room at the back the Johnnies used to sleep in the room at the back. A couple of years after I came to Leith François Olivier moved his shop or base to Maritime Street. Well, our base with François was a sort of shop, a sort of front shop, in Maritime Street, off Bernard Street in Leith. But where we were there has been knocked down now. The shop would be maybe 15 or 16 feet long. And behind it we used to have a wee kitchen, where we used to do our cooking or washing and everything. The shop was full of onions. So at that time we slept in very cramped conditions.[29]

Have you ever had rats running on top of you? Well, that's what we had in that shop in Maritime Street. I mean, you need to be really daft to live with that – but still I enjoyed it! I remember there was an old Ingan Johnny with François at that time. He was a man of maybe 55, you know. I mean, he seemed ancient to me as a boy of 14½. I cannae remember his name. But he used to snore in his bed. This night he was snoring – and this rat was in the bed beside him! You could see everything. It was really funny like, you know.

But at Maritime Street as Johnnies we slept among the onions. But you cannae smell the onions unless they're bad, they're really bad. Oh, if they're bad, aye, you could smell them! But you don't smell onions otherwise. Garlic, now that's different, I mean, the garlic needs to be really opened where it is. If you had to sleep in the same way beside the garlic I don't think that would be very agreeable because it gives you a headache. But the onions is OK. And at that time we didn't use to sell very much garlic, so we didn't have garlic so much. At that time we were only selling maybe 40 or 50 kilos of garlic in a season of five or six months between July and Christmas.

So that's how we lived – except the boss. The boss, François, always had a room to himself in Maritime Street. But us, the workers, the Onion Johnnies, always slept among the onions in the shop. There were three of us there when I began. I was easily the youngest one.

Later on my brother Jean, who was only about two years older than me, came to work there, too. I came first and Jean came afterwards. And he came with François' wife. So François and his wife were both in their own room then. They were always inside there. Some wives came with their husbands but very, very few. It was the wives of the bosses only that came, not wives of workers – they never came. Some bosses' wives stayed the whole onion-selling season but not all of them did. Some of them worked with the onions, stringing the onions, and they used to go through them, you know, to see if there were any bad onions among them and such and such. So those bosses' wives were onion workers, too. But at the most there'd only be half-a-dozen wives came.

So my brother Jean was with me at that time. He came for maybe four, five, six years. He did the job but he never came back after that. Well, I mean, he never liked the job. Well, he was not the same as me, you see. Me I can get along with everybody. I just laughed. I was just a kid then. I just played with the kids in the yard at Leith and just mixed. But Jean, a quiet lad, he would stay in a corner. And he'd gone to school, you see, and had learned English and everything like that! But he didn't like being an Onion Johnny. He never settled. He was a Johnny in Leith for maybe four or five years and then he just went back home. After that, he started to work at Roscoff in the cauliflower factory. Then after that he went for a licence for driving a long-distance vehicle. But he wasn't for coming back to Leith to sell onions.

Some of the bosses they used to make the Johnnies sign a contract. Well, you used to start sometimes at five o'clock in the morning. And there was no finishing time. You had so many strings to sell in a day – and you had to sell them. I've seen myself when I was 14½, well, maybe I was 15½, when I was with François Olivier, and I was in Musselburgh to sell onions. I went from Leith at five o'clock in the morning. And I came back again that day round about half-past ten at night.

That wasn't a normal day's work. It depended how lucky you were. But normally it was round about seven or eight o'clock at night we used to finish. Most days the leaving time from the shop or the base was from about six, half-past six in the morning. Well, you see, if you're leaving from Leith to go up to Fairmilehead, for instance, away at the furthest side of Edinburgh, with a bike full of onions, well, that's quite a long journey.

The bike loaded up with strings of onions was very heavy but, oh, you were used to it. Some of the way you cycled and some of it you walked. It depended how steep the road was. Oh, it was strenuous work, it was. And you were working until at least seven or eight at night. And sometimes, as I say, like the day I went to Musselburgh, it was half-past ten when you got home. That time I mentioned I was only 15 ½ but that could be a normal day for a Johnny, whatever your age. You were expected to do that, so you tried your best. But, you see, some days you had to come back home because you couldn't sell the onions. Then there were some days you sold all the onions and you got back a bit earlier because you were sold out. But what happened then was when you came back early, they told you, 'Well, just go out again. It's too early to finish.' You know – pay day, pay day. So if you got back home maybe at three or four o'clock they would tell you to go back again with more onions and sell them. There was a sort of working day, which was maybe from five o'clock in the morning at the earliest to maybe half-past six but, I mean, there was no right to such a thing because you were getting paid to sell so many. They were asking too much of you, you see.

That's what the pay was based on – you were expected to sell so many onions. Well, at the time I started when I was 14 ½ with François Olivier in Leith I would say it was twenty bunches of onions a day. There used to be five pound in weight in half a bunch, five pound. At that time it was 2s.6d.,

I think, for the bunch. In each bunch there would be a dozen onions, oh, easy – sometimes maybe fifteen. It depended on the sizes of the onions. So you were expected to sell about twenty bunches a day. That would be about 100 lbs of onions – maybe about 300 onions. But, I mean, that's not much.

You can't tell the number of onions you sell, you can tell the number of bunches because, I mean, you can tell by the weight. But the number of onions it varies, you see, depending if they're small or big onions. Well, as I say, you started from selling twenty bunches. After that you gradually mounted up and mounted up. By the time I was an Onion Johnny for almost twenty years – by then I'd be about 34 – I was selling sometimes 120 bunches a day.

But, you see, by that time there was a difference compared with the early years, because by that time you had vans. By then we used vans a lot. I have seen me loading on about 240 or 250 bunches inside the van. And we used to stay on until such and such a time and try to sell them. We used the van itself as a base and we cycled out from the van with loads of onions to sell. The van would be parked all day in a particular street, and as soon as you sold off your onions you came back and got more and went away back. At that time you couldn't have a driving licence before you were 21. I got a licence when I was 21, which would be about 1966 – but Onion Johnnies with another company than ours had vans before then. Maybe about half-a-dozen out of the forty or fifty Johnnies based in Leith at that time had vans when I first came to Leith in 1959. Some of them were using – well, there used to be Joseph. He had a motor bike, with a thingmy – a sort of carrier – at the front. He was alone in using that. And then a bit later on there was Henri, he used to have an old van, I think it was a Morris. Oh, I remember the old vans: the front was curved. But Henri, Joseph, and Perron – they were the first. Perron used to have a van long before we started using one, because he used to go outside of the town like, to Stirling.

Before the vans, well, you know, the Johnnies used to put their bikes on the train if they were going further off. Claude, who was my boss, my *patron*, later on, he told me when he was young he used to have so many onions to sell. And they used to put the onions in a basket or box. They used to put the box or the basket on the train and send it to wherever he was going. He used to place the basket somewhere when he got off the train, and from the basket he went out with his bike loaded with the onions. And Claude told me, too, that when he was young the Onion Johnnies actually used a pole, a baton, over their shoulder for selling their onions from on foot. That's one thing I've never seen myself. That was before my time, that's a long time ago, before the war. When I first started in 1959 I started with the bike.

In those days you woke about five or six in the morning. The boss would wake you up. You would get up and get washed and then we'd have our breakfast – bread and coffee, French coffee, French bread, and things like that. That was all. You didn't have a cooked breakfast before you went out to work – but you were entitled to it if you wanted it. But I just had some coffee and some bread.

Then you loaded up your bike with onions. You didn't do that the night before, but in the morning. Well, if you were getting up about six o'clock you were ready to go about seven. It could be seven before you actually set off, or it could be six o'clock if you were going further off somewhere. You cycled with the onions to wherever you were going.

You had a weekly round – Mondays you went to such and such, Tuesdays you went to such and such. That's how it worked. It's too far back now for me to remember where I went then, when I first started when I was 14½, on Mondays or Tuesdays or other days. But the way I work now with my van, forty years later, is exactly the same as I worked before with the bike when I was young. For instance, yesterday I was in Fairmilehead and Liberton. Tomorrow I'll be in Newington. The day afterwards I'll be in the Grange. The day after that I'll be in Church Hill and round about Bruntsfield. The day afterwards I'll be in Morningside and from Morningside I come back again to Bruntsfield. From Bruntsfield I come back down towards Ferry Road and from Ferry Road I work my way up again towards Bellevue. From Bellevue I go up Craigleith, from Craigleith I go up to the West End, and from the West End down to Ravelston Dykes. From Ravelston Dykes I go to Davidson's Mains and then to Barnton. From Barnton I go to Corstorphine, from Corstorphine I go to Balerno, from Balerno to Juniper Green, from Juniper Green to Colinton, after that Craiglockhart. Then Craiglockhart to Fairmilehead and I'm back on the same run again. From Fairmilehead I come down to Liberton. You see – it's a circle. I'm in the same place on a regular day, regular hours – Mondays I'm here, Tuesdays I'm there. It's no' very much different from what it was when I first came to Leith forty years ago.

I could go at seven o'clock in the morning to customers. Some houses in fact I do go at seven o'clock in the morning. They know me, they know I'm coming, they expect me to come at that time. They'd be disappointed if I didn't come! It was exactly the same when I used to have the push bike years ago. Monday you had your run, Tuesday you had a different run. In those days, though, it was a monthly cycle because going every week would be too often. People wouldn't eat that many onions!

I think people in Leith and Edinburgh ate about the same amount of onions as people at home in Brittany. I think what made people here in Scotland buy a bag of Breton onions was the flavour of them. It was more the flavour of them than anything else, because, you see, they're moist. Breton onions have always been moister than the Scots or English onions.

Onion Johnnies

Most of the people that buy our onions more or less stop eating their own onions. You see, our onions – it's a different flavour. I mean, the Scots or English onions as such are good. But then you've got Polish onions, which are rubbish. You know, they're really rubbish. And the Spanish onion is no' grown properly. It hasn't got time to ripen. There's too much water in it, which is no good either.

There weren't onion sellers like us Johnnies who came from Spain or Poland to sell their onions. The only Onion Johnnies were from Brittany. There was a Scottish guy who tried a wee while ago to be an Onion Johnny in Falkirk, I think. He was dressed up as an Ingan Johnny with a beret. He didn't even last a year. You need to have more guts than that. He wasn't a serious onion seller.

Well, as I say, we used to work from seven o'clock or so in the morning until seven or eight at night. You didn't have a break in the middle of the morning. Well, sometimes you stopped for a minute or two, five minutes like. But you didn't have a cup of tea or something in the middle of the morning. At lunchtime, well, we used to have a sandwich with us. We used to make up a sandwich before we left the shop in the morning and we carried it with us. Sometimes we could bring a flask with coffee with us. In the winter we used to do that. But in the summer – juice, lemonade, something like that.

Oh, very often customers would offer you a cup of tea. It did happen that customers would ask you into their house for a cup of tea. Near Ferry Road there was a house where I used to come to sell our onions on every second Saturday normally. They used to get their wages on Friday so I used to come up there on a Saturday round about twelve o'clock, always at the same time. The woman of the house used to cook fish and chips for me. People were quite kind. I always had good relations with customers, always had. I mean, people will be friendly with you if you talk to them. If you open yourself to other people, people try to understand you. They try to help you. If people don't behave like that it's because they don't know you – they make a sort of barrier, you know. But if you stick in a corner many people don't . . . It's no' because they don't want to know you. It's because they don't want to disturb you. People were polite. I mean, we'd never give them a reason to be impolite, you know. But I don't remember people being rude to me.

Well, as I say, after you had your sandwich and your coffee or your juice at lunchtime you worked on till seven or eight at night without stopping in the afternoon for a break.

You had regular customers. You wouldn't go to doors so much where you hadn't sold onions before. We had regular people that we saw. But you would try to increase the number of regular customers all the time if you could. Well, to begin with you went to every door in the street and you'd say, 'Would you like to buy onions?' But after a certain point you'd made more or less enough customers. You go for it, you know.

When I first started in 1959 I would say I had about twenty customers a day. So that would be about 120 a week, with a six-day week as it was. So when you got to that certain point, I mean, you would have about 400 or 500 customers in a month. It would vary a bit. But it didn't vary according to the time of year, it was more or less the same at whatever time of year you were going. Sometimes customers would say, 'Oh, I'm sorry. I've still got onions left. I'll not buy any today.' You would expect that, of course. Then you've got people with a family who would eat twice as much as another customer. And some others of them would only buy onions for show.

In the early years you didn't take many other vegetables with you as well as the onions – onions, garlic, shallots, that was all. Because, I mean, you were no' allowed to do anything else than that. By law you weren't allowed to do that.

I think what we were allowed to do had something to do with royalty. Later on, Claude, my other boss or *patron*, told me it began with a boat of royal people who nearly drowned at Roscoff. And I think the Onion Johnnies coming to Scotland and England started from there. You see, it was the royalty that gave their permission to the people from that corner of Brittany to come to Britain and trade their onions. That's how it began, I think. That's the corner where we all came from. The root of the Onion Johnny is in Roscoff actually. If you ever go to Roscoff, just go by the kirk – you know, the church – and if you just look at the entry of the kirk you can see there is a sort of a design of an Ingan Johnny on the kirk. Well, no' all the Onion Johnnies came from Roscoff. But that's the basis, that's where it started. And you can go all round the coast from there toward Brest – I would say maybe twenty, thirty kilometres from Roscoff. Some of them used to come from there. But Roscoff was the centre of the Onion Johnnies. Oh, Onion Johnnies have been coming from Brittany to Scotland and England for about 150 or 160 years, easy, easy. It's an old-established trade. And I think we were the only ones that were allowed to do such a thing in Britain. We didn't need to apply for a licence to sell onions. We have an Association in Brittany and it gives you freedom to come and trade in this country with onions, garlic and shallots. So we didn't have to apply to Edinburgh Town Council for a licence. We never had any kind of licence.

The Association of Johnnies in Brittany was called the *Association des Marchands d'Oignons*. It was a commercial association, not a trade union. It wasn't part of the CGT – the *Confédération Générale du Travail* – or anything like that.[30] The Association wasn't concerned with your conditions of work or your wages. The Johnnies never had a trade union as such. There's never been one in Brittany anyway. And you didn't ever think of joining a trade union in Scotland, say, like the Transport & General Workers' Union or the Farm Workers' Union or anything like that. It was a waste of time actually. They can do nothing for you. Well, I did join a union in Brittany before 1968. That was one for the factory where I worked between the onion-selling seasons. And in 1968 when there was a strike all over France the only places that weren't on strike were the vegetable factories at Roscoff. I says to the guy that was more or less the trade union official for us: 'Your trade union card,' I says, 'you can stick it wherever you like, because I don't call that a union. Everybody in France is striking but us.' So honestly I was in a trade union for nothing.[31]

You see, when the onion-selling season was finished in Scotland – that was about Christmas or early in the New Year – we used to go back home to Brittany and work in factories with cauliflowers, artichokes, potatoes, to send them to England, Holland or Germany, and things like that. We used to work in factories doing that between about January or February and July. Every year we used to go back home to those jobs in the factories. It wasn't hard to find a job because at that time there were plenty jobs. So I never did any other kind of work than work in the vegetable factory back home between the onion-selling seasons in Scotland. But I never felt at any time I would like to have thrown up the whole business of selling onions in Scotland and try to find something different. I was quite happy with the kind of work I was doing.

I don't remember suffering from homesickness, even when I first came when I was 14½, no' really. Any day, of course, it could come that, you know, you wished you would be at home in Brittany and see your pals. I did write a few letters home but no' much, not often. My mum and dad did write to me but not very often. We maybe exchanged letters three or four times in the season between July and Christmas. But I didn't write weekly letters home and my parents didn't write weekly to me either, no chance. I don't remember feeling lonely, no' really because I've always been open and friendly, as I say. If you want to make friends you can make them, you know.

I never had any contact with the French government authorities in Scotland or Edinburgh, like the French consulate. If there was any legal problem, then we would maybe be in touch but no' otherwise. I was invited only once to a reception at the consulate. It was a long time ago. I was invited because I knew the consul then. But other than that I've never had any social contact with the consulate. I've never been in the habit of going there for a glass of wine every month, no thank you!

And Onion Johnnies in Edinburgh or Leith never had much contact with other French people living in the area. It's no' that the Johnnies were a wee closed group, it was no' that. If we found French people we talked to them. If we saw somebody we knew, then we talked to them. It didnae go any further than that. It's just the same like as if we were in France, exactly the same. Oh, I had some customers in Edinburgh or Leith who were French. I had a few but I didnae have friendships with them. They were just like another customer, no more. There was maybe a chat with them about where they belonged to in France, that sort of thing. But it didn't go beyond that. You didn't get invited socially into their homes, and I wouldn't have liked that even if I had been invited. You wouldn't like to do that.

Sunday wasn't a working day, never was. When I first came to Leith François, my boss, tried to encourage me to go to church on a Sunday. I went to St Mary's, off Constitution Street. We used to go there every Sunday to mass. The other Johnnies on the whole went to church as well on a Sunday. After mass we sometimes used to go on a Sunday to the pictures. I think they were open then on a Sunday evening.[32]

Either that or I used to go on Saturday evening to the pictures. I know I used to go, every week I used to go to the pictures. Normally you were entitled to finish work earlier on a Saturday. You would finish, I would say, about six o'clock and then you would go out. We used to go as well to the dancing in Edinburgh. I used to go to the Cavendish, the Palais de Danse and, I think, the Locarno – out towards the Cattle Market.[33]

One day I was at the dancing – it's a long time ago – and there was a guy had been stabbed in the back at the dancing. And the police were there, some of them at the door, not letting people out and as we came towards the police I says to the police, 'We're Ingan Johnnies,' I says. 'Let us go. We had nothing to do with it.' The police knew us. No Onion Johnnies have ever been in the police records here. Nobody was ever in trouble. We were all honest and law-abiding, we never had any fights or incidents like that. I mean, rather than fighting we would run away from it, you know. One day I was going to the dancing again and this guy just came up to me and he says, 'You're a Roman Catholic.' I says, 'Yes.' You could see hate in his eyes, you know. That's the first time I'd seen that, sectarian people. But I just walked away from him.

Well, I stayed working with François Olivier four-and-a-half or five years, I think. Then I went to work with Claude Tanguy because, you see, you've got bosses who will try to learn you. Some bosses don't want you to learn, because the more you learn, the more you earn respect from them, which is quite normal. So I went from François to Claude. Claude was very good because he learned me everything.

I learned even to phone here after I had been some time with Claude. By that time I had a car. My car was in the garage. I says to Claude, 'Can you phone the garage and see if the car is ready?' He says, 'You don't know how to phone?' I says, 'No,' I says, 'I've never phoned.' 'Well,' he says,' 'it's easy, see. You pick up the handset, you dial your number and you put the penny in, you see.' At that time I think it was 2d. And so that was the first time I learned to use the phone.

Onion Johnnies

When I was working with François we didnae use to go to the pictures during the week. We only started to go during the week when we were with Claude. You see, when we were with Claude sometimes there was a sort of agreement. I'd say to him, 'Can I go to the pictures?' 'Aye,' he says, 'OK, you go.' But the next again day he says, 'Can you do this for me?' It worked both ways. I would say to Claude, 'Tomorrow we'll wake up an hour earlier. I want to see the film, so I'll get up a wee bit earlier tomorrow to make up for what I lose.' Claude was very understanding. And no' only that, he respected the person as a whole. I mean, if he had something to say he just said it to your face. And that was it – finished. But François, he wasn't the same. He was more for himself – and more frightened that anything might happen to you as well: accidents. Claude was more relaxed towards those kinds of things.

So when I was talking to Claude, you see, it's always, 'I'm learning, I'm learning, I'm learning.' Claude would advise you if you were doing right or wrong. You know, he would tell you, 'You should do this, you should do that.' I used to listen to him and sometimes we used to argue as well. Everybody who knew him would tell you the same as me. He was really a genuine person. Oh, Claude was about thirty years older than me. He was like, well, he was no' ma dad. You know, you've got your parent. But I would say Claude would have been my second dad. Claude and me stayed friends until he died. He died about 1992 or '93. When he died I was working here in Edinburgh so I wasn't at his funeral.

François Olivier was the same age as Claude but François was no' so helpful as Claude. François would let you do your job and that's as far as he would go. I mean, you could ask him questions and he would answer. But to put you on the right way, rather than having you ask – no, no. François was different totally from Claude. Both of them belonged to Roscoff.

Claude's base, his shop, in Leith was in Sandport Street. We didnae sleep among the onions there. The top shop was for storage of the onions and for working. At the back we used to have a kitchen. And in the kitchen we used to have three beds. We used to sleep in the same room – Claude, me, and my brother Jean when he was there. And there we used to have a toilet, as we'd had in Maritime Street with François as well. It was a flush toilet. Otherwise you wouldn't have been allowed to live in the shop, no' with the government here in Edinburgh, no chance.

By the time I left François to go and work with Claude I was about 19 or 20 and I was getting only £60 a month from François – £15 a week. I cannae remember if that's exact but it was more or less like that. When I first started with François, when I was 14½, I was getting £40 a month maybe – about £10 a week. That was for about a 12– or even 14–hour day, six days a week – say, about 70 up to 84 hours a week anyway. But, you see, Claude offered me I think it was £80, something like that. It was a real rise, much more than I'd got from François. But I went to work with Claude not only for that but because there was more freedom with him as well. And then at the end of the onion-selling season Claude would show if he was happy with your work. He would give you a few extra pounds, well, no' an extra few pounds – quite a wee bit extra. I've seen him doing it. Well, it could go up to £200 more. François wasn't like that. Well, it was maybe no' François, it was his wife, you see. His wife was involved as well. You see, when you've got a woman involved it's very, very hard like.

By the way, the only woman Onion Johnny at Edinburgh or Leith I ever heard of was the daughter of a boss. I never saw her, I never met the woman actually because it was before my time. I just heard about her. I think she was just a young girl who came over maybe, maybe just for a season or two. But she was the only woman I ever heard of working as an Onion Johnny.[34]

Onion Johnnies

If an Onion Johnny was married and had a family in Brittany, he wasn't seeing them for half the year. But that's the way they lived. I don't think the Johnnies suffered from loneliness or homesickness, no' as such. They were brought up like that. Oh, it's never been easy for their wives at home. But they came to expect that. The Johnnies and their wives had been brought up like that as well. And, you see, at that time it wasn't only the Onion Johnny that was going away from home. As I say, my dad, too, a farm worker, went away from home to the sugar beet near Paris for maybe two months at a time when I was young. So, you see, we had been brought up like that. We had to move sometimes, to go away from home for times. There was no other choice.

Well, I worked with Claude between ten and fourteen years. Then Claude couldn't come back to Scotland any more because he had arthritis. He could hardly walk. So he had to stay at home.

Claude gave me advice to go into partnership with another Onion Johnny, Louis Guyader. He and I used to work together with Claude. So we did that. I would say Louis was, oh, ten or twenty years older than me. So he and I worked in partnership. We organised the transportation of the onions from Brittany. But by that time there was no shipping any more, the boats had stopped coming to Leith and the onions came by road. And it was costing you more. But that was just the way it was, it was the only way you could get the onions. So they came by lorry from Roscoff – by that time I think they had the Brittany Ferries – and they came to Plymouth, and then up the motorway from Plymouth. I was in partnership with Louis for about five, six years until Louis had to stop as well. He just wanted to stop. He was getting too old as well.

By that time there were far fewer Onion Johnnies coming to Scotland. It must have happened about 1975. The people were too old. And there were no young ones taking their places. The young ones don't want to work as we did.

Younger people didn't want to work the long hours that the Onion Johnnies worked. It wasn't anything to do with the Common Market or changes in the law. And younger people were finding work in factories and things like that at home in Brittany or elsewhere in France. So the number of Onion Johnnies in Leith and Edinburgh was much smaller. After a time there were only five or six. And then maybe three or four years after that – phew! That was it. So from, I would say, about 1985 I was the only Onion Johnny here. By then all the other Onion Johnnies had retired or weren't coming back to Scotland. Most of them were retiring age, you know, and they didn't sort of like coming still and doing the work. That was a big change, because Onion Johnnies had been coming to Scotland for about 150 years.

In a sense it was sad. But, I mean, life goes on. I wouldn't say the job became easier for me because there was no longer any competition when I became the only Onion Johnny. Competition has never been bad. It is better to have competition than none at all. Of course, it makes you realise that you've got to sell good quality, because if a customer is no' happy and if there is no competition he just wants to take the stuff and no' grumble. But if you have something you sell and the customer is no' happy and there is competition, then automatically the customer is going to go to the other man. And you ask him why and he says because the quality is better, price is better, and such and such. So, as I say, competition has never been harmful.

In the old days, there was respect between the Onion Johnnies. The Johnnies didn't each have their own special areas for selling the onions. Let's say you could actually have three or four Onion Johnnies all working on one route, things like that. It wasn't that the Johnnies got together and sort of agreed 'You do that and I'll do this', oh, no, no. As I say, you could find yourself coming along the same street with two or three other Onion Johnnies, all trying to sell your onions –

and talking amongst each other. The only thing the Johnnies disliked was if there was one of them lying, telling lies to a customer. That's the one thing nobody among the Johnnies liked. So if you did tell lies you'd be better to hide yourself, because the other Onion Johnny would come to you and tell you you had been telling lies. He would because, I mean, nobody likes lies. There was maybe comradeship among the Johnnies – let's say after work, but during work, no. There was no such thing. There was competition, there really was. But that didn't spoil your relations with the other Onion Johnnies, there was no nastiness or bitterness. Once the work was finished, well, that was it. And then, you see, we used to see each other at home around Roscoff as well.

I got married in 1988. My wife's from Mauritius. We met in Brittany. She lives here in Edinburgh with me. We have one child.

I would like to remain working in Edinburgh as long as I can. That's what I've done all my life. When I feel I've had enough and want to retire I would go back home to Brittany. It's no' that I don't like it here in Scotland. I do like it here but, you see, the thing is you've got your roots. And you go back to your roots. I'm no' saying I would retire in Brittany but I would go there for a certain period to see if I can settle there. You never know if you can settle because, I mean, I've been away from home half my life. So it's very hard to tell. It's like the opposite of what I did when I was 14½ and first came to Scotland. When I first came I didn't know how I would cope with the job as an Onion Johnny. It's worse now because the way we live now and the way we used to live then is totally different. In France, too, there have been big changes. I mean, if you go back there and you don't see your friends because they're not there, well, you've got nobody. So you've got to start from point blank. In that case you might say, 'Oh, to hell. I'll just go back to where I was in Scotland.'

I remember Mrs Lily Berry, who was a friend of mine. She died not long ago, well, maybe about 1996 or '97. She used to stay at Willowbrae in Edinburgh. And I remember her saying to me, 'You're going to be the last Ingan Johnny in Edinburgh'. I said, 'No way, no way. I'll no' be the last one.' And it happened. You never can tell what's going to be in your life.

NOTES

1 In the case of Northern Ireland, Jean-Marie Tanguy recalls hearing his father say that there the Johnnies' onions had been stolen from them. 'I don't know but I think it was because the Johnnies were Bretons and Catholics that they had difficulties in Northern Ireland. So only one or two Johnnies tried to sell onions there but they didn't succeed.' See above, p. 119.

2 See the Appendix below.

3 Thomas Johnston, *The History of the Working Classes in Scotland* (Glasgow, n.d.), 356, where the Midlothian Farm Workers' Protection Society's demands in 1872 were said to include one that 'wages were to be paid weekly, not every six months.'

4 See above, p. 37 Yves Rolland, the only Johnny so far as is known who continues to work in Scotland, indicates that if he found it impossible to settle into eventual retirement in Brittany, he might return to live in Scotland. See above, p. 164.

5 Albert Ernest Pickard (1874–1964), 'the last of Glasgow's great eccentrics', a Yorkshireman who described himself as 'A.E. Pickard Unlimited of London, Paris, Moscow and Bannockburn', began as a printing worker then apprentice engineer, became a repairer of penny-in-the-slot machines, then a showman with his own stalls in several European cities. Arriving in Glasgow in 1904, he set up an 'American Museum', became owner of two theatres, and during the 1914–18 War built his first cinema in Townhead, and became a property millionaire, second in the extent of his ownership only to Glasgow Corporation. He attempted unsuccessfully several times to become a city councillor, and stood unsuccessfully also in the 1951 parliamentary election as 'The Independent Millionaire Candidate' in Maryhill Constituency, when he came bottom of the poll with only 356 votes. He had several residences but died in a fire in one of them at Belhaven Terrace, Glasgow, in October 1964. *Glasgow Herald*, 31 Oct. 1964; Carol Foreman, *Glasgow Curiosities* (Edin-

burgh, 1998), 127–37; Joe Fisher, *The Glasgow Encyclopedia* (Edinburgh, 1994), 118; Jack House, *The Heart of Glasgow* (London, 3rd ed. 1978), 91–3.

6 Maurice Chevalier (1888–1972), French music hall performer and film star, a prisoner of war in 1914–18, who was described in 1930 as 'the highest paid talkie artist in the world'. *Glasgow Herald*, 2 Dec. 1930. Jean Milin's recollection is clear but, despite a systematic search, no report of any performance in Edinburgh by Chevalier between 1930 and 1936, when Monsieur Milin returned to France, has been found in the local press.

7 The rate of exchange of the franc in 1930 was about 124 to the £. See, e.g., *Glasgow Herald*, 3 Dec. 1930.

8 Hitler's forces seized Narvik in their invasion of Norway on 9 April 1940 but were driven out briefly from the town at the end of the following month by a Franco-British expeditionary force which, however, was withdrawn on 7 June because of the impending collapse of France itself in the face of the German invasion there. B.H. Liddell Hart, *History of the Second World War* (London, 1973), 51–63.

9 Of the 338,226 men who were rescued in the 'miracle of Dunkirk' between 26 May and 4 June 1940, 120,000 were French. 'Unfortunately a few thousand of the [French] rearguard were left – and this left sore feelings in France . . . It [the evacuation] was an amazing result compared with earlier expectations, and a grand performance on the part of the Navy.' Liddell Hart, *op. cit.*, 79–80; Peter Young, *World War 1939–1945* (London, 1966), 65.

10 Marshal Philippe Pétain (1856–1951), hero of the defence of Verdun in the 1914–18 War, became head of government at the fall of France in June 1940. The armistice his government signed with Nazi Germany on 22 June included the division of the country into an Occupied and an Unoccupied Zone. The zone occupied and administered by the Germans was the northern half of France, including Paris and extending as far south as Tours and Dijon, plus a broad band of territory on the Atlantic coast right down to the Pyrenees. Alsace and Lorraine were annexed entirely to Germany. The remainder of France – the Unoccupied Zone – was controlled by the French government headed by Pétain, which had its base at Vichy. Pétain collaborated with the Germans in the hope that his Vichy state would become a political partner of Nazi Germany. At his meeting with Hitler on 24 October 1940 at Montoire, Pétain agreed that Vichy and the Axis Powers (Germany and Italy, the latter of which had entered the war on 10 June 1940 against France and Britain)

'have an identical interest in seeing the defeat of England accomplished as soon as possible. Consequently, the French Government will support, within the limits of its ability, the measures which the Axis Powers may take to this end.' After the war, Pétain was tried and convicted of treason and sentenced to death, but the sentence was commuted to life imprisonment, and he died in prison at the age of 95. William L. Shirer, *The Rise and Fall of the Third Reich* (London, 1970 ed.), 815, quoting the text of the Montoire Agreement.

11 The Alhambra, at 200–204 Leith Walk, had opened in 1914 as a theatre before it became a cinema. Closed in 1958, the building was demolished in 1974. Other cinemas that existed in Leith during Anna Gourlet's years there were the Alison, Laurie Street (1911–1946), Gaiety, Kirkgate (1913–1944), Palace, Constitution Street (1913–1966), Capitol, Manderston Street (1928–1961), and the State, North Junction Street (1938–1972). *Edinburgh Evening News*, 7 Mar. 1958 and 9 Jan.1974; Sandy Mullay, *The Edinburgh Encyclopedia* (Edinburgh and London, 1996), 71–2.

12 John Cormack (1894–1978), born in Edinburgh, son of a Baptist lay preacher, served, 1909–22, in the Argyll and Sutherland Highlanders, including in Ireland, where he seems to have become rabidly anti-Catholic. He founded in 1933 the Protestant Action movement, which won considerable support in Leith and subsequently gained several seats on Edinburgh town council. In 1934 Cormack himself was elected a councillor for North Leith ward. Organiser of a mass protest against the Catholic Eucharistic Congress in Edinburgh in 1935, Cormack was tried, fined and briefly imprisoned for inciting a riot the following year during the visit to the city of Monsignor Ronald Knox (1888–1957), a prominent Catholic theologian and writer. Though Cormack lost his seat in the town council in 1937, he was returned the next year for South Leith and remained a councillor until he retired in 1962. Appointed a bailie in 1955, he had been fined £3 two years earlier for breach of the peace arising from one of his regular open-air meetings at the Mound. *Edinburgh Evening News*, 21 Oct. 1961 and 4 Aug. 1969; *Scotsman*, 22 Nov. 1984; R. Gording (ed.), *Chambers Scottish Biographical Dictionary* (Edinburgh, 1992), 94–5; Tom Gallagher, *Edinburgh Divided. John Cormack and No Popery in the 1930s* (Edinburgh, 1987).

13 The French navy, the most powerful in Europe after that of Britain, had not suffered defeat, unlike the French army and air force, in June 1940. The armistice that month provided that,

Notes

apart from some vessels committed to protecting French colonial
interests, the French navy was to return to its home ports, most
of which were in the Occupied Zone, there to be demobilised and
disarmed under the control of Germany or Italy. Both these
powers declared they would not use French warships for their
own purposes – but that declaration seemed likely to prove
worthless. From the point of view of the British government,
faced with the threat of invasion after the collapse of France, it
was vital that the French navy, most of whose modern warships
had sailed to North Africa in time to avoid capture by the
Germans, should not fall into the hands of the latter. Some
French warships berthed at Portsmouth and Plymouth were
seized by Britain on 3 July, and many members of their crews
volunteered to fight on against the Axis Powers; another French
warship squadron at Alexandria agreed next day to become
demilitarised peacefully; but the refusal of a strong squadron at
Oran and Mers-el-Kebir in Algeria to accept any from among a
choice of proposals from the British government intended to
ensure these warships did not fall into German or Italian hands
resulted in their bombardment on 3 July by a British squadron,
the destruction of or serious damage to several of the French
ships, and the loss of 1,297 lives among their crews. A few days
later French warships at Dakar in West Africa were attacked
unsuccessfully by British naval forces, and the attack, assisted
this time by Free French troops of General de Gaulle, was
renewed toward the end of September 1940, but again unsuccessfully. In fact, no French warships were used by the Germans or
Italians against Britain and its allies in the course of the war.
When in November 1942, in swift response to the Allied landings
in North Africa, the Germans invaded and seized the Unoccupied
Zone in France, what remained of the once-powerful French fleet
was scuttled at Toulon to prevent it falling into their hands.
Winston Churchill, *The Second World War*. Vol. II (London,
1949), 201–12; Captain S.W. Roskill, *The Navy at War* (London,
1960), 80–1, 83–6, 107–9; Young, *op. cit.*, 226–7; Robert O.
Paxton, *Vichy France* (New York, 1972), 6–7, 42–356–7, 70–1,
110–13, 280–1.

14 Even before the outbreak of the 1939–45 War and Italy's entry
into it in June 1940 at the time of the collapse of France,
Mussolini had claimed that Corsica, Nice and Tunisia should
be added to his Fascist empire. Mussolini's regime in Italy was
brought to an end in July 1943, and although the new Italian
government signed an armistice with the Allied powers on 3

September, Rome and northern Italy were promptly occupied by the Germans. That same month Sardinia, however, fell to the Allies, without a shot fired, and Free French troops from North Africa were landed in Corsica, from which the Germans then evacuated their garrison to Italy. Paxton, *op. cit.*, 254; Roskill, *op. cit.*, 325–6, 337.

15 St Mary's RC Primary School register for these years appears to contain no entry for François Perron, although it records the attendance at the school between September and December 1931 of Jean Creach, the son of another Onion Johnny, whose address was The Store, Elbe Street, Leith.

16 After the limited success of the *relève* scheme agreed between the Vichy government and Nazi Germany in June 1942 by which for every three skilled French workers volunteering to work in Germany one French prisoner-of-war there would be released, the ruthless Nazi demands for foreign forced labourers led to entire age groups of young Frenchmen being conscripted to work in German factories from February 1943 through the Service du Travail Obligatoire. Thousands of young Frenchmen avoided this forced labour by joining the *maquis* (which literally meant scrubland or bush – to take to the scrub or bushes meant to join the underground, the Resistance to Nazi occupation of France), whose activities undertaken from their camps in the mountainous areas of France included raiding offices of the STO and burning their files of conscripts. Henri Michel, *The Shadow War. The Resistance in Europe 1939–45* (London, 1972), 267–77; Paxton, *op. cit.*, 292–3, 310–11, 322.

17 T. Robertson Mossman, of Marshall & Mossman, estate and property agent and valuer, 125 Constitution Street (at 20 Leith Walk before the 1939–45 War). *Edinburgh and Leith Post Office Directory 1959–60* (Edinburgh, 1959), 318, and *1938–9* (Edinburgh, 1938), 374.

18 Young, Glover & Co. Ltd, fruit brokers, 10 Bernard Street, Leith. *Edinburgh and Leith Post Office Directory 1938–9, op. cit.*, 575.

19 Gumley was almost certainly either Lindsay D. Gumley, JP, Glebe Road, Cramond, or Charles S. Gumley, WS, White House, Cammo Road, Barnton, who had lived at those addresses since before the 1939–45 War. *Edinburgh and Leith Post Office Directory 1939–40* (Edinburgh, 1939), 209, and *1959–60, op. cit.*, 179.

20 Between seasons 1946–7 and 1952–3, when their forward line was for most of the period the 'Famous Five': Gordon Smith, Bobby Johnstone, Lawrie Reilly, Eddie Turnbull, and Willie

Ormond, Hibs were Scottish Division I champions in 1947–8, 1950–1, and 1951–2, and runners-up in 1946–7, 1949–50, and 1952–3, and finalists in the Scottish Cup, 1947. G. Docherty and P. Thomson, *100 Years of Hibs 1875–1975* (Edinburgh, n.d. (1975)), 93–103, 125; Mullay, *op.cit.*, 121.

21 See above, Note 16. As Eugène Guyader indicates, the maquis or Resistance group he joined was not in the mountainous regions of south-eastern France but in Brittany itself.

22 General Charles de Gaulle (1890–1970), leader of the Free French in the 1939–45 War, head of the French government, 1944–46, president of the Fifth Republic, 1958–69. The cross of Lorraine with its distinctive two horizontal cross-pieces, the upper shorter than the lower, was adopted as the emblem of the Free French during the war.

23 McCaig's Folly or Tower was built between 1895 and 1900 at a cost of £5,000 by an Oban banker, John Stuart McCaig, as a replica of the Colosseum in Rome. The Tower was intended to form a monument to his family but McCaig died before building was completed. Frank A. Walker, *The Buildings of Scotland: Argyll and Bute* (London, 2000), 411; John Keay & Julia Keay (eds), *Collins Encyclopedia of Scotland* (London, 2000), 779.

24 Either the referendum held in Oct. 1946 or, perhaps more likely, the consequent election held the following month for the new National Assembly appears to be the event Claude Quimerch refers to. The second Constituent Assembly submitted to electors in the referendum a draft constitution for the Fourth Republic, and the draft, which proposed a two-chamber parliament in which the second chamber had little power, was passed by 9,120,576 votes to 7,980,333 votes, with a further 7,938,884 voters abstaining from voting. Thus the constitution of the Fourth Republic was approved by a 53 per cent majority of those who voted, but by only a minority of the total electorate. In the parliamentary elections in November the Communist Party gained almost 300,000 votes and secured a total of almost 5½ million – the largest number won by any party in the election. David Thomson, *Democracy in France since 1870* (Oxford, 5th ed., 1969), 237; Alexander Werth, *France 1940–1955* (London, 1957), 324.

25 On 7 December 1966 in Glasgow Celtic beat Nantes 3–1 in the return match in the second round of the European Cup, making the aggregate score in their two matches Celtic 6, Nantes 2. The attendance at the match at Celtic Park was 41,000. Celtic later beat Inter Milan 2–1 in the final of the Cup. *Glasgow Herald*, 8

Dec. 1966; Brian Wilson, *Celtic: a century with honour* (London, 1988), 135.

26 For extracts from Guy Le Bihan's diary, see Appendix below.

27 Peter Saddler & Co. Ltd, stevedores and warehousekeepers, 4 Bernard Street, Leith. *Edinburgh and Leith Post Office Directory, 1959–60* (Edinburgh, 1959), 385.

28 Admiralty Street ran southwards from Commercial Street toward North Junction Street. The present much shorter Admiralty Street runs northward from North Junction Street into Cromwell Place.

29 Maritime Street, running between Queen Charlotte Street and Bernard Street, and almost parallel with Constitution Street, follows more or less exactly the line of the former Quality Street.

30 Confédération Générale du Travail, or General Confederation of Labour, founded in 1895 – the principal French trade union organisation.

31 France in 1968 was one of the centres of a huge wave of student protest movements and workers' strikes that occurred in many parts of the world in that and the following year. There were major riots and confrontations between protesters and police, particularly in Paris in May 1968. The movement almost brought down General de Gaulle as President of the Fifth Republic – he retired the following year. See, e.g., Eric Hobsbawm, *Age of Extremes. The Short Twentieth Century, 1914–1991* (London, 1994), 444–9.

32 Opening of cinemas on Sundays in Edinburgh had begun following a decision by 47 votes to 14 by Edinburgh town council in December 1953 to allow two cinemas in the city to open on Sundays between 4.30 p.m. and 10 p.m. for an experimental period of six months. 'The Edinburgh and South-East Scotland section of the Scottish branch of the Cinematograph Exhibitors' Association gave evidence that 13 of the 23 cinemas in Edinburgh had indicated they would definitely open on Sundays if permission were granted, three would not, and seven were "uncertain".' *Scotsman*, 6 Dec. 1953.

33 The New Cavendish was at West Tollcross, the Palais de Danse in Fountainbridge, the Locarno Ballroom in Slateford Road, and the cattle market at Chesser Avenue. *Edinburgh and Leith Post Office Directory 1962–3* (Edinburgh, 1962), 869, 955.

34 This is presumably a reference to Anna Gourlet, Onion Johnny or 'Jenny' in Leith in the 1930s. See above, pp. 57–65.

APPENDIX

Guy Le Bihan's diary notes, September-December 1977

During the autumn of 1977, in what proved to be his last but one year as an Onion Johnny in Scotland, Guy Le Bihan kept notes in a small pocket diary of his journeys and sales of onions in Ayrshire and elsewhere in the west and south-west of Scotland. A photocopy of these notes is preserved in the National Library of Scotland (Acc. 12024). The following are translated extracts from the first few pages of Guy Le Bihan's notes:

8 Sep.: Ayr 100 bunches. Finished 3.30 p.m. Ayr 20 bunches, finished 6 p.m. Fine weather.

9 Sep.: Kilmarnock. Irvine Rd, Shorles, Belfield. 153 bunches. Finished 7 o'clock. Hurlford 18 bunches, Monkton 9 bunches. Rain.

10 Sep.: Beith 160 bunches, Gordon 8 bunches. Finished 5.30 p.m. A little rain.

11 Sep.: Ballantrae 22 bunches, 7 lbs garlic. £15, £7. 1st week: 473 bunches.

12 Sep.: Newton Mearns 152 bunches. Finished 7.15 p.m. Fazzi–garlic 215 lbs x 75 = £161; onions 5 bunches. Fine weather.

13 Sep.: Troon 152. Finished 6.30 p.m. Fine sunny weather.

14 Sep.: Prestwick 150. Finished 5.50 p.m . . . Foggy.

15 Sep.: Whitecraigs, Giffnock 150 bunches. Finished 6 p.m. Fine weather.

16 Sep.: Kilmarnock, Glasgow Rd 152 bunches. Finished 7.30 p.m. Fine weather, cold in the morning.

17 Sep.: Kilbirnie 151. Finished 7.50 p.m. Bistrot Dalry 12, remainder Kilwinning. Fine weather, white frost. Gordon 2, Christine 3.

Sold the second week: 912 bunches.

19 Sep.: Largs 80. Skelmorlie 70. Butcher 20 bunches x 70. Garlic Lugano 15 lbs x 80, Riviere 6 lbs x 80, Royal Hotel 12 lbs x 80. Finished 6 o'clock. Fine sunny weather.

20 Sep.: Saltcoats, Ardrossan 150 bunches. Finished 7.10 p.m. Fine weather, overcast.

21 Sep. Girvan, Maybole, Ayr. Monument Rd behind Callan. 146 bunches. Finished 7.30 p.m. Very hard. Racing at Ayr. Fine weather, overcast.

22 Sep.: White Craig orchard. Hill Park. 144 bunches. Finished 7 o'clock. Fine weather, overcast.

23 Sep.: Largs, Fairlie, West Kilbride, Saltcoats. 144 bunches. Finished 7.30 p.m. 3 x 7 lbs Piklin. 2 x 5 lbs.

24 Sep.: Catrine, Mauchline, Hurlford, Darvel, Newmilns. 140. Finished 6.30 p.m. Remainder Ayr 32 bunches. Gordon 2 bunches. Overcast weather.

Sold the third week 876 bunches.

26 Sep.: Dundonald, Irvine, Ayr with 42 bunches. 140. Finished 7.30 p.m. Rain in afternoon, evening very bad.

27 Sep.: Newland 136 bunches. Finished 6.30 p.m. Rain in afternoon, not too bad.

28 Sep.: Cambuslang, Rutherglen, Low Burnside. Breakdown Victoria Bridge from 11 a.m. until 5 o'clock. Sold 84 bunches. Finished 8 o'clock. Remains 56 [bunches]. Storm, rain, a deluge on the return.

29 Sep.: Netherlee, Simhill [?], Burnside, Rutherglen 140 bunches. Finished 6.40 p.m. Rain all day.

30 Sep.: Cumnock 45, Alloway Rozelle, Maybole Rd, to left. 140 bunches. Finished 8 p.m. Torrential rain until 6 o'clock, then fresher and drier.

1 Oct.: Stranraer 140 bunches. Finished 4.15 p.m. Mr Thom-

son 6 + 6 beside Hotel 4. [Foin? – hay] 8 bunches. Not too hard. Terrible weather – rain, hail storm, wind.

Sold the 4th week 820 bunches. Sold in all 270 sacks [of onions].

3 Oct.: Clarkston, Busby, Carmunnock 136 bunches + 4 sacks. Finished 6.20 p.m. Rain all day.

4 Oct.: Bearsden 178 bunches. Finished at 8 p.m. Remains 17 bunches. Very hard, doleful. Morning – rain, afternoon – fine weather.

5 Oct.: Maxwell, Cathcart. 136 bunches + 1 sack. Finished 7.30 p.m. Fine weather, rain in the evening to 9 o'clock.

6 Oct.: Ayr, Doonfoot, Seafield, Midton Rd, Welch, Dalmellington Rd. 136 bunches + 2 sacks + 2 Picklen. Finished 6.40 p.m. Fine weather, colder.

7 Oct.: Kilmarnock, Irvine Rd, Shorles, Bellfield, Hurlford (12). 136 bunches. Finished 7 o'clock. Rain all day long, flooding at Glasgow.

8 Oct.: Beith. 136. Finished 4.30 p.m. Gordon 8. 136 + 8 = 144. Fine weather.

Sold 5th week 806 bunches, 7 sacks, 2 Picklen.

. . . [Sold] 1st week 473 bunches
2nd week 912 bunches
3rd week 876 bunches
4th week 820 bunches
5th week 806 bunches
6th week 737 bunches
7th week 742 bunches
8th week 727 bunches
9th week 605 bunches [All Saints Day, 1 November, this week]
10th week 736 bunches
11th week 816 bunches
12th week 828 bunches
13th week 935 bunches
14th week 124 bunches [Only two days worked in this week].

INDEX

176

Index

Index

Index

Onion Johnnies, 1–175 *passim*; ages at becoming, 2, 3, 4, 5, 7, 8, 9, 12, 13, 15, 22, 23, 24, 26, 27, 30, 32, 42, 43, 44, 57, 58, 59, 66, 67, 68, 75, 77, 78, 79, 89, 95, 106, 109, 110, 112, 122, 124, 143, 146, 149, 150, 157, 161, 164; ambitions of, 4, 5, 40, 55, 67, 77, 90, 111, 124, 142, 164; area in Brittany from, 5, 6; areas and distances covered by, 12, 13, 14, 22, 26, 27, 31, 38, 39, 40, 45, 47, 48, 49, 57, 59, 60, 63, 66, 69, 71, 75, 80, 85, 86, 97, 99, 100, 101, 114, 116, 129, 130, 135, 150, 152, 153, 173–5; Association of, 6, 38, 73, 156; bases of, 8, 9, 10, 13, 14, 25, 27, 31, 33, 36, 37, 38, 44, 54, 58, 59, 67, 68, 73, 75, 76, 78, 84, 85, 86, 88, 95, 96, 106, 113, 115, 119, 124, 144, 145, 146, 147, 148, 161, 170; batons or poles used by, 12, 13, 24, 26, 33, 36, 46, 47, 48, 59, 60, 70, 79, 113, 152; bicycles used by, 12, 13, 14, 27, 31, 33, 36, 38, 39, 40, 45, 48, 49, 50, 60, 69, 70, 79, 80, 85, 86, 97, 99, 113, 114, 129, 150, 151, 152, 153; Bretons only, 154; camaraderie among, 18, 38, 45, 73, 121, 164; carrying of onions by hand by, 13, 59, 60; companies of, 3, 7, 8, 9, 10, 11, 13, 14, 16, 28, 33, 34, 37, 40, 44, 57, 58, 66, 73, 77, 80, 83, 85, 89, 96, 106, 113, 119, 124, 125, 128, 129, 145, 151; competition between, 11, 18, 28, 29, 40, 62, 80, 83, 86, 87, 127, 128, 129, 134, 163, 164; contacts with home by, 18, 117, 132, 133, 157, 162; contacts with French officialdom of, 158; contracts of employment of, 108, 149; credit and, 18, 30, 51, 101, 102; diary of, 14, 131, 172, 173–5; frequency of rounds of, 18, 30, 48, 71, 85, 101, 114, 130, 152, 153; generational occupation for, 2, 3, 4, 11, 19, 22, 23, 57, 66, 76, 77, 89, 110, 111; handcarts used by, 12, 13, 26, 27, 31, 33, 36, 47; Irish seasonal workers and, 17; language difficulties of, 18, 24, 27, 30, 50, 78, 113, 125, 147, 159; law-abiding, 159; living and sleeping conditions of, 8, 9, 10, 16, 25, 26, 36, 37, 38, 39, 41, 44, 46, 58, 59, 68, 78, 85, 86, 96, 100, 113, 115, 124, 130, 146, 147, 148, 161; motor cycles used by, 13,

113, 151; numbers of, 2, 8, 9, 11, 17, 25, 28, 34, 38, 44, 59, 73, 77, 78, 80, 81, 85, 89, 96, 113, 119, 124, 125, 128, 129, 144, 145, 148, 151, 161, decline in, 1, 5, 18, 19, 37, 40, 83, 86, 133, 134, 135, 162, 163; only one remaining, 1, 5, 163, 164, 166; origins of, 6, 77, 155, 156; other employments of, 17, 106, farmer, 11, 22, 17, 75, 89, 110, 111, 120, 135, farm worker, 17, 82, 83, 113, 132, lorry driver, 90, 91–4, 95, 105, 109, 149, sugar beet, 17, 107, transport worker, 68, in vegetable factory, 17, 66, 84, 87, 149, 157, vegetable packer, 28, 32, 36, 40, 57; other vegetables sold by, 5, 18, garlic, 6, 30, 70, 81, 82, 101, 106, 126, 129, 148, 155, 156, 173, 174, piclels (piklin or picklen), 70, 174, 175, shallots, 6, 30, 81, 82, 155, 156; partnerships of, 162; *patrons* (bosses) and *ouvriers* (workers) among, 3, 6, 10, 11, 14, 15, 16, 25, 26, 28, 37, 44, 45, 46, 47, 68, 77, 78, 95, 96, 106, 108, 109, 113, 145, 148, 149, 152, 155, 158, 159, 160; public attitudes to, 17, 18, 49, 61, 63, 71, 72, 81, 86, 97, 98, 99, 117, 131, 154, 155, 158; retrospective views of, 41, 56, 65, 74, 88, 106, 107, 121, 135, 164; sales techniques of, 18, 24, 25, 29, 31, 34, 47, 53, 61, 62, 72, 97, 101, 113, 114, 119, 120, 125, 126, 127, 130, 153, 154, 155; seasonal nature of work of, 1, 2, 5, 6, 7, 8, 16, 17, 22, 24, 28, 32, 43, 46, 57, 67, 68, 74, 75, 78, 82, 84, 87, 89, 105, 109, 112, 120, 132, 135, 144, 148, 149, 157; state pensions of, 40, 74, 84, 87, 106; on their own, 11, 66, 74, 119, 128, 145; traders' licences and, 6, 73, 155, 156; travel from Brittany by, 2, 6, 7, 8, 24, 43, 57, 58, 77, 78, 95, 105, 106, 112, 113, 143, 144, 146; use of trams or trains by, 13, 14, 27, 33, 38, 45, 49, 60, 85, 152; vans or cars used by, 13, 14, 37, 39, 40, 80, 85, 86, 95, 97, 99, 100, 113, 114, 129, 130, 151, 152, 153; wives of, 2, 4, 5, 7, 8, 16, 19, 22, 23, 32, 37, 41, 55, 57, 58, 59, 62, 63, 64, 65, 66, 67, 68, 74, 75, 76, 78, 84, 86, 87, 88, 95, 107, 108–9, 111, 112, 120, 122, 131, 132, 133, 134, 135, 149, 161, 162, 164, Scottish, 17,

181

Index